CREATING FRACTALS

CREATING FRACTALS

ROGER T. STEVENS

CHARLES RIVER MEDIA, INC.

Hingham, Massachusetts

Editor: David Pallai
Cover Design: Tyler Creative
Cover Images: Roger T. Stevens

CHARLES RIVER MEDIA, INC.
10 Downer Avenue
Hingham, Massachusetts 02043
781-740-0400
781-740-8816 (FAX)
info@charlesriver.com
www.charlesriver.com

This book is printed on acid-free paper.

Roger T. Stevens. *Creating Fractals.*
ISBN: 1-58450-423-4

Library of Congress Cataloging-in-Publication Data
Stevens, Roger T., 1927-
  Creating fractals / Roger T. Stevens.
    p. cm.
  Includes bibliographical references and index.
  ISBN 1-58450-423-4 (pbk. with cd-rom : alk. paper)
  1. Fractals. 2. Curves. I. Title.
  QA614.86.S734 2005
  514'.742—dc22
                        2005004791

Printed in the United States of America
05 7 6 5 4 3 2 First Edition

CONTENTS

INTRODUCTION

By the beginning of the 20th century, scientists, especially physicists, knew enough about the laws of physics and how they governed the universe so that they began to feel that everything in this field was already known. There were just a few curious things that didn't fit too well that needed to be cleared up and the book of physics could be marked complete and closed forever. Unfortunately, in clearing up these odds and ends, whole new fields evolved, such as the behavior of electrons and quantum mechanics. Soon physicists were shocked by a whole new conception of the universe and new discoveries that totally changed our way of life. Suddenly, physics was in a state of revolution, with more unanswered questions than ever before. Alfred North Whitehead, the American mathematician and philosopher, was fond of pointing this out; he felt that one of the most significant aspects of this revolution was what its effect would be on the philosophical outlook of physicists. Never again would they take the smug, self-contained attitude that everything was known and complete. Instead, their minds would always be open to the myriad of possibilities of the unknown.

Unfortunately, this open-minded attitude did not last very long. By 1980, physicists were postulating that we already know everything about physics that is important in daily life and that future discoveries would require huge sums of money and large machines to discover insignificant refinements. Anyone who owns a pen that is not only a writing instrument but can be connected to a computer as a 256-megabyte hard drive knows how wrong these predictions were. In fact, a whole revolution in scientific thinking had already begun that would cut across disciplinary boundaries so that physics, as well as other sciences, would never be the same again. This revolution is called *Chaos* theory. In essence, this new field finds that many of the things we had believed about the orderly behavior of equations are often untrue. We now know that some very simple iterated equations can result in very complex patterns of behavior. Furthermore, for some of these equations, improving the accuracy of the input data, rather than improving the accuracy of the solution, causes the equations to take a completely different path that diverges widely from the previous result. We now have to take a new look at the whole field of mathematical solutions.

For centuries, mathematicians were comfortable with an intuitive feeling for what might happen when they wrote down systems of equations. A simple set of equations would produce simple results. In most cases, the result would be a simple, stable expression that represented the end state of the system. If things got a little more complicated, the equation might blow up, meaning that there were unfortunate sets of inputs for which the result would head toward infinity. In other situations, the result might be a periodic function, which would never reach an end value, but would at least settle down to a regular repeating function that could be easily predicted. In the real world, situations existed where the state of a system could not be predicted at any given time. Mathematicians got around this problem by representing the system state through the selection of random numbers. They often referred to the system as noisy, where noise was a function that took on completely random values, over a given range, through time. Supposedly, noise represented the results of some regular functions that we did not yet know how to define and measure. As soon as our understanding and methods improved a little more, we could fully understand, characterize, and eliminate (if necessary) the effects of noise.

"Monster" Curves

The belief in the totally ordered structure of mathematics first began to fall apart in the late 19th and early 20th centuries, when mathematicians such as Georg Cantor, Helge von Koch, and Giuseppe Peano began to draw curves quite unlike those that mathematicians had ever seen before [Cantor32] [vonKoch05] [Peano73]. These curves were often undifferentiable. They were usually self-similar (the shape of each small segment of the curve was the same as the shape of a much larger segment), their length could not easily be measured or defined, and their dimension appeared to differ from the traditional dimension of one for a line and to be perhaps somewhere between a line and a plane.

Traditional mathematicians called these curves "monsters" and "pathological" and refused to deal with them at all. Most of these strange curves were the result of repeated iterations of certain types of equations. Cantor, von Koch, and Peano continued to try to analyze these equations, but lacking the tools of modern computers, they spent many years performing manual calculations without making much progress.

Working with Fractals

Fractals is the name given to certain types of iterated equations that produce very strange results and are capable of creating some very unusual and beautiful patterns. Dr. Benoit Mandelbrot, a researcher at IBM who was one of the first to use modern computers to process iterated equations, created this name [Mandelbrot83]. One of the unique aspects of fractals is that they seem to defy conventional notions of the meaning of dimension. A line is supposed to have one dimension, but a fractal line can be drawn to wind around in such an intricate path that it ultimately fills the entire plane on which it is drawn. This kind of behavior has resulted in a new definition of *dimension,* which goes beyond the old one and can have a floating-point value greater than 1 rather than just an integer value to describe the space-filling capability of a curve. In the next chapter (Chapter 2) we shall attempt to answer the question, "What are fractals?," and to give you some idea of their nature and how to use them. The heart of this book is a Fractal program that allows you to generate thousands of different kinds of fractals, to enlarge them, to color them, and to save them. You can do this with a few simple commands; you don't need any detailed knowledge of computers or computer programming. Your artistic efforts using this program are limited only by your own talents. In addition, the chapters that follow describe the characteristics and mathematical background of each fractal and show you how the program works to produce each one.

THE LORENZ AND OTHER STRANGE ATTRACTORS

The chaos revolution really began about 1961. Edward Lorenz, at the Massachusetts Institute of Technology, was attempting to develop a model for weather systems that would make improved weather forecasting possible [Lorenz93]. His model appeared to be a fairly good representation of weather patterns. When run on a computer, it produced results similar to the kind of weather that actually occurred.

The computer that Lorenz was using was pretty slow and his time on it was limited, so he made a practice of periodically recording his results so he could continue when he got more computer time. One day, Lorenz wanted to pick up from the middle of a previous computer run and examine a sequence in greater detail. He typed in his intermediate data and started the program again. To his dismay, the new computer run started by duplicating the results of the previous one, but then began to diverge farther and farther from the previous results. Lorenz satisfied himself that these results were not because of a faulty computer and ultimately determined that the cause was that he had typed in the intermediate results to only three decimal places, whereas the computer had been using six decimal places.

This appeared to be bad news for weather forecasters; if over a period of weeks weather patterns could be completely different because of differences in the fourth or higher decimal places of input data, there appeared to be little possibility that forecasters could collect accurate enough data to make accurate long-range forecasting possible. Lorenz eventually reduced his model to three simple differential equations, which also happened to represent fluid flow or the action of a particular type of water wheel. The result of these equations, over time, was not a single stable result or a periodic function. But it was not random noise, either. Instead, a curve appeared that was ordered and predictable, but differed drastically depending upon the initial conditions. Basically, regardless of input, this set of equations settled down to values from within a family of curves. Fortunately, the curves took on a set of predictable values; unfortunately, the curves continued on to infinity without ever repeating themselves. These curves became known as the *Lorenz attractor*. It was the first of the strange attractors. The mathematics of the Lorenz equations is described in detail in Chapter 3. By selecting the *Lorenz Attractor* fractal type in the Fractal program, you can view the resulting strange attractor. The Lorenz attractor is a three-dimensional figure. The program allows you to view it as an isometric projection or as a projection on any two of the three available planes. Chapter 3 also gives a full description of another strange attractor that you can view with the Fractal program.

WHAT YOU CAN DO WITH L-SYSTEMS FRACTALS

Next, we are going to look at a whole family of fractals known as L-Systems fractals. They start with an *initiator*, a simple line or geometric figure (such as a triangle or square). There is also a *generator*, a pattern of lines that can be scaled, oriented, and used to replace each line of the *initiator*. Then another iteration can be performed wherein each line of the figure that was just produced is replaced by a smaller copy of the generator. As many iterations as desired can be produced, each showing more and more detail, until the detail becomes so small that your computer monitor is no longer capable of showing it. The name *L-Systems fractals* comes because this class of fractals can be easily programmed using the *L-Systems* computer language, which Aristid Lindenmayer developed as a convenient way to model plants [Prusinkiewicz90]. By using the basic approach and adding a few special touches, you can use this language to create all the L-Systems fractals that are described in this book. This includes many fractal patterns that were previously produced using much more complicated methods (including manual calculation for some of the early ones).

Although L-Systems can produce lovely and interesting patterns that have all of the characteristics of fractals, they are not capable of the infinite amount of varied detail that can be produced by iterated equation fractals. These, and how to use them, will be described in later chapters. Chapter 4 introduces an overview of the L-Systems fractals and describes what you can do with them. This is basically limited to color changes and to enlargement when desired.

THE SNOWFLAKE AND OTHER VON KOCH CURVES

Chapter 5 begins by describing a very familiar L-Systems curve, the von Koch snowflake [vonKoch05], which uses a triangular initiator and a generator having four line segments, each one-third of the original line length. The first and last of these trace along the first and last thirds of the original line. The other two lines of the generator are also each one-third of the original line length. They are positioned so that they and the original middle third of the original line form an equilateral triangle. This chapter also describes other von Koch curves that include the quadric von Koch curves (which are so called because the generator is a square), and a number of other interesting fractal patterns. The von Koch curves are self-similar, that is, an enlarged portion of the curve shows the same general shape as the originally sized curve, as we could have anticipated because they are created by using the same generator line pattern at smaller and smaller scales. They are also self-avoiding, that is, as the curve is drawn, it never touches any portion of the previously drawn part of the curve.

PEANO CURVES

Another family of fractals that can easily be created using the L-Systems approach is the Peano curves [Peano73]. These differ from the von Koch curves in that they are not self-avoiding. The curve touches itself at various points, so it is sometimes difficult to determine just what the path is. Most Peano curves have a fractal dimension of 2, indicating that they eventually fill the whole plane on which they are drawn. This makes them useful as a pattern for scanning a two-dimensional graphic. Chapter 6 describes these curves in detail and shows how some of them can be modified to allow the user to clearly visualize the path of the curve.

GENERATORS WITH DIFFERENT LENGTH LINE SEGMENTS

Thus far, the fractal curves that have been described use a generator that consists of a number of line segments of equal line length. Many more intricate and beautiful fractals can be created if the equal length feature is not a requirement. A generator can start with a number of equal length line segments, the line length may change for the next one or more line segments. The remainder of the generator may then have line segments of the same length as the original generator line segments. Chapter 7 shows three beautiful fractal curve families, each of which is created by replacing one line of a generator by a different pattern of lines of a different size.

THE HILBERT CURVE

Until now, the curves being considered were produced by a method called *edge rewriting*, in which each line of a figure is replaced by a generator pattern of lines. Fractals in which the figure becomes more complex can be drawn by inserting a generator pattern in between the junction of every two lines in the current figure. This is known as *node rewriting*. This can also be done using the L-Systems approach, but it is more difficult because the size of the figure changes significantly at each level. The Hilbert curve is one of these curves [Hilbert27]. Chapter 8 describes this curve and how it is drawn.

FASS CURVES

Another family of fractals that can easily be drawn using the L-Systems technique is called FASS curves, because they are space-*F*illing, self-*A*voiding, *S*imple, and self-*S*imilar. Various FASS curves can be drawn using either the edge-rewriting or node-rewriting technique. Chapter 9 describes how to produce these curves.

TREES

As mentioned earlier, the L-systems technique was first developed by Lindenmayer to describe the geometric structure of plants. Fractal curves that have the typical branching structure of trees and bushes can be drawn using the L-Systems capability to draw part of a pattern and then return to an earlier point in the pattern and branch off in a different direction. Chapter 10 describes a number of trees that are created with the L-Systems capability of the Fractal program. These are all stick trees; that is, branches and trunks are all drawn with lines of minimum thickness. A thickness parameter can be added to all the branches and even to add flowers and leaves, but our Fractal program does not include this capability.

CREATING YOUR OWN L-SYSTEMS FRACTALS

A table containing the pertinent L-System inputs needed to create the fractal accompanies each of the fractals described in Chapters 5 through 10. The L-systems technique is a language that can be conveniently used to describe the initiator and generator of a fractal of the type that begins with the initiator and then repeatedly replaces each line segment with a pattern of lines called the generator. As with all languages, it is convenient shorthand for describing reality, and it can be conveniently manip-ulated by a computer to create the actual fractal drawings. You don't have to be a programmer to make use of the L-Systems language because the Fractal program is designed so that you can enter the desired parame-ters of any new fractal of this type that you want to create and the pro-gram will take care of putting it into the L-Systems language for you. Chapter 11 shows how you can select from the menu of fractal types the heading *Create L-Systems Curve*. This causes the program to display a table into which you can enter the proper values to create your own L-Systems fractal—thus, your fractal-creating capability is limited only by your own imagination. To gain experience in this, you can choose one or more of the fractals in Chapters 5 through 10 and enter its parameters into the table. Once you've tried this with several of the already specified L-Sys-tems fractals, you are ready to create your own. After entering the de-sired parameters, you can select the desired level and then click *Close*, whereupon the fractal will be displayed. When you've created a fractal that you especially like, be sure to save the parameters so that you can re-create it whenever you want to.

NEWTON'S METHOD

Newton's method is a well-known mathematical method for using iteration to zero in on the actual roots of an equation such as

$$f(z) = 0 \tag{1.1}$$

which starts with a guess about what the root might be [Newton11]. When these iterations are plotted, some very interesting fractal curves re-sult. The Fractal program enables you to produce very interesting fractal pictures showing the results of applying Newton's method to the equation:

$$n - 1 = 0 \tag{1.2}$$

Chapter 12 describes this technique in detail and points out some in-teresting discrepancies in the boundary regions.

FRACTALS WITH THE LOGISTIC EQUATION

In the early 1970s, Robert May, at the Institute for Advanced Studies at Princeton, was looking at the mathematics of population growth. The critical equation was

$$x_n = rx_{n-1}(1-x_{n-1}) \tag{1.3}$$

This simple equation had been assumed to have two outcomes: either a population achieved a stable equilibrium value or it tapered off to extinction. As May experimented with different values of the parameter r, however, a strange phenomenon occurred. As the parameter grew larger, the result ceased to achieve a stable equilibrium and instead began to oscillate between two different values. A little larger value of the parameter created 4 alternating stable states, then 8, and so forth until the behavior became chaotic and didn't settle down to any value at all. But then, as the parameter increased some more, a stable window was found in the middle of chaos, with three alternating states that then increased to 6, 12, and finally back to chaos again. Another window, farther on, began with 7 alternating states.

May's friend James Yorke, at the Institute for Physical Science and Technology at the University of Maryland, did a rigorous mathematical analysis of the behavior of this equation and proved that if a regular cycle of period three ever occurs in any one-dimensional system, then the same system will also display regular cycles of every other possible length and various completely chaotic cycles as well. Yorke and Tien-Yien Li wrote a paper on this, which was mischievously called *Period Three Implies Chaos* [Li75]. This is the origin for the name chaos in this new field of science.

A few years later, Mitchell Feigenbaum was studying the same equation at the Los Alamos National Laboratory [Feigenbaum78]. He observed a regularity in the period doubling effect, which had a ratio of 4.6692016090, now known as the *Feigenbaum number*. Strangely enough, this same ratio applies to period doubling in a wide variety of iterated equations; almost any iterated equation for which the basic equation produces a curve with a hump.

Chapter 13 describes several interesting applications of the logistics equation. The first is the interesting fractal that occurs by simply plotting the logistics equation for different values of r. This is known as the bifurcation diagram. It is also possible to treat this equation as a Julia set. Chapters 13 and 14 describe how Julia sets are created, detailing the unique way in which the iterations are performed and how colors are used to create beautiful Julia displays. With the right choice of c, a dragonlike fractal is created. Dragon curves are fractals that have the appearance of a mythical dragon. They can be displayed using a set of yellow, red, and orange colors to increase the dragon likeness. Chapter 13 shows how this is done. Finally, Aleksandr Lyapunov, a Russian mathematician, discovered the formula for an exponent that, when applied to a dynamic system, gives an indication of how chaotically the system is behaving. Mario Markus applied this technique to the logistics equation and worked out a method for creating a display in which coloring was based on the value of the Lyapunov exponent [Markus89]. This technique is fully described in Chapter 16. A number of interesting Lyapunov fractals can be created using the Fractals program.

MANDELBROT AND JULIA SETS

In the 1970s, Mandelbrot at IBM's Thomas J. Watson Research Center, was taking a closer look at the von Koch and Peano curves [Mandelbrot83]. A technique had been developed years before for assigning a dimension greater than the standard Euclidian dimension to such curves. This dimension is known as the *Hausdorff-Besicovitch dimension* [Hausdorff19] [Besicovitch29]. Throughout this book, it is also called the *fractal dimension*. Mandelbrot coined the term "fractals" to describe all curves whose Hausdorff-Besicovitch dimension is greater than their Euclidian dimension. Mandelbrot was looking in depth at the equation

$$z_n = z_{n-1}^{\,2} + c \qquad\qquad (1.4)$$

where z and c are complex numbers. Mandelbrot developed a new way of mapping this equation: the *Mandelbrot set*. This fractal is obtained by allowing c to be set in turn to the complex number represented by each point on the display screen and then iterating the equation for a predetermined number of iterations (the default being 128 in our program). If the point settles down to a steady value, it is assigned a base color. If the point goes off toward infinity, it is assigned a color based on how many iterations are required for it to become larger than a predetermined value (the default being 4.0 in our program).

The Julia set uses the same equation, but c remains constant while z_0 is in turn assigned a unique value for each pixel on the display. The Julia set also uses a different coloring scheme, in which the base color is assigned to all points that go off toward infinity, and other colors are assigned to those points that don't, the color being based on the value that the point finally settles down to.

One unique characteristic of Mandelbrot and Julia sets, and of other sets created by a similar iteration technique, is that when enlarged, new fractals appear that are similar to but still quite different from the original sets. Furthermore, this process of enlarging to create additional detail seems to go on indefinitely. Chapter 14 is an overview that shows how you can use the Fractal program to produce new, beautiful enlarged Mandelbrot and Julia fractals.

Not all choices for the value of c in the Julia set turn out to produce interesting fractals. In fact, many of them result in a totally blank screen.

However, the Mandelbrot set turns out to be a kind of catalog of all possible Julia sets, from which particularly interesting Julia set parameters may be selected for mapping. Sharp changes in tracing the perimeter of the Mandelbrot set often correspond to values for c that result in interesting Julia sets. The Fractal program enables you to right-click on a point in the Mandelbrot set that looks like it might represent the right parameters for an interesting Julia set. The program will then create a Julia set with these parameters. An overview of how this is done is included in Chapter 14. Chapter 15 describes the mathematics of the Mandelbrot and Julia sets and shows how to create many examples of these fractals.

WORKING WITH COLORS

So far, we've described some very basic methods for assigning colors to Mandelbrot and Julia sets. In addition, the Fractal program has a lot of other ways of using colors. Not all of these color combinations are compatible with every type of fractal, so you do have to use a little caution. For example, all of the L-Systems colors are drawn with a foreground color on a background. The default values of these colors are black for the fractal and white for the background. By using the *Select Color Combination* menu, you can select *Color Background* to choose your background color and *Image Color* to choose your foreground color. But don't select the same color for both or else your fractal will be invisible. Special color combinations can be chosen for dragon curves and for Phoenix curves (the Phoenix curve will be described in Chapter 20), and a color combination of blues and silvers works very well with Mandelbrot and Julia-like fractals. The *Random* setting randomly selects a palette of 16 colors and the *Random Julia* setting uses these randomly selected colors on Julia sets. You can also use the *Set Custom Colors* command to pick the exact colors that you want for a 16-color palette. Once you have selected these, you can use them for any suitable fractal by using the *Use Custom Colors* or *Use Julia Custom Colors* command. The *Gradient* menu item uses a set of 1024 shades of color that by default goes from blue through gold, yellow, and white and then back to blue again. The *Modify Gradient* button at the right of the screen brings up a display that allows you to fully manipulate the gradient. The *Default Gradient* menu item allows you to get back to the default set of gradient shades at any time, no matter how much manipulation you have done. There is a special set of colors for showing the complexities of the default Newton fractal and a special set of colors for Binary Decomposition. There are also three sets of complex colors that often produce startling three-dimensional effects. Finally, there is a set of 400 shades varying across the rainbow for displaying the Lyapunov fractals. All of these are described in detail in Chapter 16.

CURVES FROM TRIGONOMETRIC AND EXPONENTIAL FUNCTIONS

Once you have become familiar with the Mandelbrot, Julia, and dragon curves, you'll begin to realize that these are just scratching the surface of available fractals. A number of equations given in many mathematical reference books can be used to create interesting and unusual fractal patterns. Especially interesting and unusual fractals can be developed using iterated equations that involve trigonometric or exponential functions. The Fractal program includes a number of these, which are described in Chapter 17.

FRACTALS USING ORTHOGONAL FUNCTIONS

It turns out that interesting fractal curve families can be based on the iterated use of one of almost any family of orthogonal functions. Many of these are listed in standard mathematical reference books. The Fractal program includes a large variety of these. The interesting thing about using these equations is that their default representations look very similar to the Mandelbrot set, but as you zoom in on tiny portions of the picture the detail become completely different, but equally exciting. These fractals are described in Chapter 18.

Selecting the menu item *Create 2nd to 7th Order Equation* allows you to write your own fractal equation. This requires a little more expertise than is needed for other fractals of this nature. First, not all equations produce good fractals. If you select an orthogonal polynomial from a book of mathematical functions, your chances of getting a good fractal are better, but not perfect. Finally, you have to enter everything in the appropriate boxes in proper format. For example, if you enter an alphabetic expression where a double floating-point number is required, the program will crash. Using this capability is described in Chapter 19. It gives you almost unlimited flexibility in creating this type of fractal.

PHOENIX CURVES

The *Phoenix* curve is supposed to look like a pair of phoenixes rising from the ashes. Discovered by Shigehiro Ushiki at Kyoto University, it is based on an iterated equation that is unusual because it incorporates the current value of the variable being treated and its value from the previous iteration. Full details on this curve are given in Chapter 20.

THE MANDELA FRACTAL

The Mandela fractal is created by iterating the following equation:

$$z_{n+1} = 1/z_n^2 \qquad (1.5)$$

If we use the standard Julia coloring schemes with this fractal, the result is a rather uninteresting set of concentric circles. However, if we select our color to be one of an array whose index is taken as the integer value of the real part of z, we have the beautiful fractal that is called the Mandela. How this is done is described in Chapter 21.

POKORNY FRACTALS

The Pokorny fractals are created by iterating the following equation:

$$z_{n+1} = 1/(z_n^m + c) \qquad (1.6)$$

where n can be any integer. The Pokorny fractals have $n + 1$ symmetrical points. They are very beautiful, but you shouldn't make the exponent too large or much of the beauty is lost. You can try a large exponent and then expand a small portion of the resulting display to see what effects occur, however. These fractals are described in Chapter 21.

FRACTALS USING CIRCLES

Circles can be used as the basis for some very interesting fractals. However, neither the L-Systems language nor the program for generating Mandelbrot-like or Julia-like fractals is suitable for producing circular fractal patterns. Instead, we need to have tailored software for each circular application. Chapter 22 describes three types of circular fractals, *Apollonian packing of circles*, the *Pharaoh's breastplate*, and the *self-homographic fractal*. The Pharaoh's breastplate begins with computing a number of circles and then uses an interesting mathematical transformation called inversion to create the final fractal. Both the untransformed and transformed patterns can be displayed using the fractal program. The self-homographic fractal uses a different mapping transformation that results in a beautiful detailed fractal.

BARNSLEY FRACTALS

Michael Barnsley, a mathematics professor at Georgia Tech, has discovered several fractals in which the iteration equation changes for the next iteration depending on the value of the variable that is obtained from the current iteration [Barnsley88]. Chapter 23 describes several of these fractals, which can be displayed by the Fractal program.

ITERATED FUNCTION SYSTEMS

Barnsley has also investigated Julia sets, looking for ways to produce even more variability and, perhaps, to generate patterns that matched those of living things. Barnsley discovered what he called *iterated function systems* [Barnsley88].

Basically, such a system consisted of several sets of equations, each of which represented a rotation, a translation, and a scaling. By starting with a point and randomly applying one of his sets of equations, according to specified probability rules, Barnsley could generate classic fractals, and he soon discovered how to make the rules for generating ferns and other shapes from nature. This technique is described in Chapter 24. The chapter includes the parameters used to generate a number of iterated function systems (IFS) fractals. Once you become familiar with how this is done, you can select *Iterated Function Systems* from the *Select Fractal type* menu and then *Create Your Own IFS* from the submenu. This will allow you to enter your own set of parameters to generate an IFS fractal that has never been seen before.

MIDPOINT DISPLACEMENT FRACTALS

Suppose we start with an initiator such as we use to begin an L-Systems fractal, but instead of replacing each of its sides with a generator, we find the midpoint of each initiator line and connect the midpoints together. If we started with a triangle, for example, this process would result in four smaller triangles. We can repeat for many iterations, but the resulting fractal is not a very exciting picture. However, suppose that after generating each midpoint, we perturb it by moving its location in some random manner. After a number of iterations, the result is a fractal that looks like a section of terrain. This technique is particularly useful in generating pictures of mountains. Chapter 25 describes how this is done.

CONTINUING ON YOUR OWN

ON THE CD

In this chapter, we've given you a brief overview of the fractals and other contents of this book. Now you're ready to proceed to work with fractals directly. The Fractal program on the accompanying CD-ROM will give you all kinds of flexibility in creating, enlarging, coloring, and saving thousands of fractal pictures. If you also want to know something about the mathematical characteristics of certain fractals and how their displays are created, you can find this in the chapter devoted to whatever type of fractal is of interest to you. Although there are occasions where special fractal characteristics need to be designed into the program, there are so many different opportunities available using the Fractal program as it stands that you should be able to fully satisfy your creative urges and develop new fractals that have never been seen before. Also, bear in mind that a number of interesting discoveries about the basics of mathematics have come out of experimenting with and developing new fractals. You might discover one of them.

REFERENCES

[Barnsley88] Barnsley, Michael, *Fractals Everywhere*, Academic Press, Inc., 1988.

[Besicovitch29] Besicovitch, A. S., "On Linear Sets of Points of Fractional Dimensions," Mathematische Annalen (1929): Vol. 101.

[Cantor32] Cantor, G., *Gesammelte Abhandlungen*, edited by E. Zermelo, 1932. Reprinted by Georg Olms Publ., 1962.

[Feigenbaum78] Feigenbaum, Mitchell J., "Quantitative Universality for a Class of Nonlinear Transformations," Journal of Statistical Physics (1978): Vol. 19, No. 1.

[Hausdorff19] Hausdorff, Felix, "Dimension und ausseres Mass," Mathematische Annalen (1919): Vol. 79.

[Hilbert27] Hilbert, David, "The Foundations of Mathematics," in *The Emergence of Logical Empiricism*, Garland Publishing, Inc., 1996. (Article originally published in 1927.)

[Li75] Li, Tien-Yien, and Yorke, James A., "Period Three Implies Chaos," *Transactions of the American Mathematical Society* (December 1975): pp. 985–992.

[Lorenz93] Lorenz, Edward N., *The Essence of Chaos*, University of Washington Press, 1993.

[Mandelbrot83] Mandelbrot, Benoit B., *The Fractal Geometry of Nature*, W. H. Freeman and Company, 1983.

[Markus89] Markus, Mario, and Hess, Benno, "Lyapunov Exponents of the Logistic Map with Periodic Forcing." *Computers and Graphics* (1989): Vol. 13, No. 4, pp. 553–558.

[Newton11] Newton, Isaac, *De analyst per aequationes numero terminorium infinitas*, 1711.

[Peano73] Peano, G. *Selected Works of Giuseppe Peano*, 1973.

[Prusinkiewicz90] Prusinkiewicz, P., and Lindenmayer, A., *The Algorithmic Beauty of Plants*. Springer-Verlag, 1990.

[vonKoch05] von Koch, Helge, *Une methode geometrique elementaire pour l'etude de certaines de la theorie des courbes planes*, 1905.

WHAT ARE FRACTALS?

The development of modern high-speed computers has made possible the investigation of certain techniques involving fairly simple equations that when iterated a large number of times produce results having complex and often beautiful characteristics. The resulting mathematical sets have qualities that have caused us to rethink our conventional notions of how mathematics is applied to the real world. The name *fractals* was created by Dr. Benoit Mandelbrot, a researcher at IBM who in the 1970s did the first extensive computer work on such mathematical sets [Mandelbrot83]. If a curve has a Hausdorff-Besicovitch dimension that is larger than its Euclidian dimension, Mandelbrot defined it as a fractal [Hausdorff19] [Besicovitch29]. Mandelbrot created the word fractal from the Latin adjective *fractus*. The Latin translations can mean *fragmented* (as in *fraction* or *refraction*) or *irregular*, both of which are characteristics of fractal curves. This gives an overall view of how Mandelbrot looked at fractals. He believed that just as Euclidian geometry was the proper tool for delineating man-made objects, so fractal geometry was the proper tool for delineating the objects of nature; they are characterized by fragmentation and many irregularities. To understand the meaning of the definition of a fractal through its dimensional characteristics, we need to look at an example. Draw a line on a sheet of paper. Euclidean geometry tells us that this is a figure of one dimension, namely length. Now extend the line. Make it wind around and around, back and forth, without crossing itself, until it fills the entire sheet of paper. Euclidean geometry says that this is still a line, a figure of one dimension. But our intuition strongly tells us that if the line completely fills the entire plane, it must be two dimensional. This paradox caused the mathematicians Felix Hausdorff and Abram Besicovitch to redefine *dimension*, making it a measure of space-filling capability. They came up with some mathematical techniques for computing the Hausdorff-Besicovitch dimension for various types of curves. From here on, we will refer to this dimension as the fractal dimension. So one characteristic of fractals is that they generate lines that are so convoluted that they appear to have a dimension greater than the Euclidian one.

ITERATED FUNCTIONS

Consider the following iterated equation:

$$x_{n+1} = f(x_n) \tag{2.1}$$

This is representative of many situations in mathematics where a solution is found by iteration. The hope is that by arbitrarily selecting an initial value for a variable and plugging it into the function a new value will be obtained that is closer to the actual value of x. This new value, in turn, is inserted into the function and another value of x is obtained that is even closer to the actual value. After a sufficient number of iterations, the value obtained for x zeroes in on the actual value. Before the days of digital computers, a lot of manual effort was required in using this process with sufficient iterations to obtain a workable solution. However, even with these limitations, it began to appear that iterated equations were not as well behaved as mathematicians would like. Mathematicians such as Georg Cantor, Helge von Koch, Giuseppe Peano, Felix Hausdorff, and Abram Besicovitch drew curves that were called "monsters," "psychotic," and "pathological" by traditional mathematicians. But without high-speed digital computers, the actual drawing of such curves was a long and tedious process. So little progress occurred in this unusual field for nearly a hundred years.

The advent of digital computers made the investigation of such curves a fruitful field. Multiple iterations became quick and simple. We could look at the work from a hundred years ago and extend it. One thing became obvious that cast a shadow on conventional mathematical techniques. It had always been assumed that if we had some fairly accurate data and plugged it into an equation, the resulting answer would be a fairly correct and useful result. Then, if our input data became more accurate, the answer would come closer to the "real" value of the result. But some fractal equations were found to have what is called *sensitivity to initial conditions*. When initial data was plotted, and then changed by a very insignificant amount (for example, in the third decimal place) the entire plotted curve would diverge widely from that previously plotted. So what is the "real" result? We don't really know. We don't even know for sure how accurate the input data must be to get the result we want.

In working with iterated equations, performing iterations many times and plotting the resulting location of the parameter at each state also showed that fractals had other interesting characteristics. For one thing, they never repeated themselves. For another, they were not differentiable. Furthermore, they tended to have the characteristic of self-similarity. In other words, if a small portion of the plot was enlarged, its shape was very much like a large portion of the original plot. Finally, iteration of a very simple equation could result in plots that seemed to have infinite detail. Each time a section of the plot was enlarged, more, different, and unsuspected detail was revealed. Some of these plots turned out to have shapes of great interest and extreme beauty, offering all sorts of potential for artistic achievement.

As we have pointed out, when the first of these curves was investigated, traditional mathematicians called them "monster" curves, and mostly refused to deal with them at all. We know a lot more about fractals now, but we're still far from explaining all the strange behavior associated with them.

HOW ARE FRACTALS USED?

Now we have explained what a fractal is, but explaining how a fractal is used is a little more difficult. We've mentioned that Mandelbrot contends that just as the shapes of traditional geometry are the natural way of representing man-made objects (squares, circles, triangles, etc.), fractal curves are the natural way of representing objects that occur in nature. Thus, fractals have a value both as art objects and as a means of representing natural scenes. Moreover, fractals occur naturally in the expressions for mathematical phenomena as varied as the predictions of weather systems, the descriptions of turbulent flow of liquid, and the growth and decline of populations. Fractals are also useful in dimensional transformations that can be used for expressing and compressing graphical data. If we ignore the artistic value, the best answer to the question "What are fractals good for?" is the reply "Fractals appear to provide solutions to many previously unanswered questions at the frontiers of the physical sciences." Consequently, to work at the frontiers of science, one needs to understand what fractals are and how to work with them.

This book includes a program that will run on any computer equipped with Windows and will enable you to create, enlarge, color, and save a wide variety of fractals. The program can be used for artistic creation, but it is also designed to give you some understanding of the characteristics of each fractal produced. The later chapters describe each fractal type, including information about its mathematics and how the fractal picture is calculated. You don't need any computer knowledge to create thousands of beautiful pictures, but we've also included some categories that extend your fractal-creating ability, but need a little skill to use properly. Just ignore these categories until you feel confident of your ability to work with the program.

BASIC CONSIDERATIONS

Let's establish some points of orientation that will be useful in practical investigations into the chaotic field of fractals:

1. Intuition leads us to believe that fractal curves should have a dimension greater than their traditional geometric dimension. As described in the following section, the Hausdorff-Besicovitch, or fractal dimension, meets this requirement and gives us a handle on the dimensionality of a fractal.
2. Fractal curves are associated with many physical and natural phenomena.
3. Fractals often possess extensive detail and a rare and unusual beauty. No doubt, this is partly true because fractals correspond to the way in

which nature produces those shapes that we are most familiar with and that basically define our ideas of "the beautiful."

4. Fractals have the unusual characteristic that they can be defined totally by relatively simple mathematical equations, yet they are not periodic. Thus, the progression of the fractal curve may differ widely if we start at just slightly different points in space, so unless we can measure where we are with absolute precision, we cannot be sure just what the progression of the curve will look like—even though the curve is defined through all its wanderings by very simple iterated expressions.

5. Most fractals are self-similar, so that the shape that we identify in the plot of a fractal curve repeats itself on a smaller and smaller scale that can be seen only as we enlarge the image further and further.

FRACTAL DIMENSIONS

Let's return to the statement made at the beginning of this chapter that a fractal is a curve whose Hausdorff-Besicovitch dimension is greater than its Euclidian dimension. We now have some idea of the nature of fractal curves and of what this new definition of dimension means, but that doesn't help much unless we can actually come up with some meaningful dimensional numbers. A rigorous definition of the Hausdorff-Besicovitch dimension is a rather lengthy mathematical process, and for many fractals, it is almost impossible to determine this dimension. However, for a large class of self-similar fractals, which we will discuss in later chapters, the fractal dimension is easily obtained. Suppose that we start with an *initiator* that is some simple geometric figure consisting of a number of connected line segments. It may be a triangle or a square or even just a straight line. We now define a *generator*. This generator is a series of line segments that is going to replace every line segment of the initiator. The generator consists of N line segments, each of whose length is the length of the line segment being replaced multiplied by r, where r is the fraction of the line segment being replaced. The arrangement and length of the N line segments is such that the distance from the beginning of the generator to its end is the same as the length of the line segment being replaced. The replacement process repeats an infinite number of times, each time replacing each line segment of the previous level curve with a scaled-down replica of the generator. It can then be shown that the Hausdorff-Besicovitch dimension of the resulting fractal curve is

$$D = \log N \,/\, \log(l/r) \qquad\qquad (2.2)$$

where N is the number of line segments in the generator and l/r is the fraction of the original line length compared with the length of the line being replaced. Comparing this dimension with the Euclidian dimension gives us some idea of the properties of a fractal. For example, a D of 1.0 is simply an ordinary line, whereas a D of 2.0 means that the curve completely fills the plane. With this background in mind, let's begin looking at fractal curves and the software to view them and work with them on any computer running a recent version of Windows.

REFERENCES

[Besicovitch29] Besicovitch, A. S., "On Linear Sets of Points of Fractional Dimensions," *Mathematische Annalen* (1929): Vol. 101.

[Huasdorff19] Hausdorff, Felix, "Dimension und ausseres Mass," *Mathematische Annalen* (1919): Vol. 79.

[Mandelbrot83] Mandelbrot, Benoit B., *The Fractal Geometry of Nature*, W. H. Freeman and Company, 1983.

3

THE LORENZ AND OTHER STRANGE ATTRACTORS

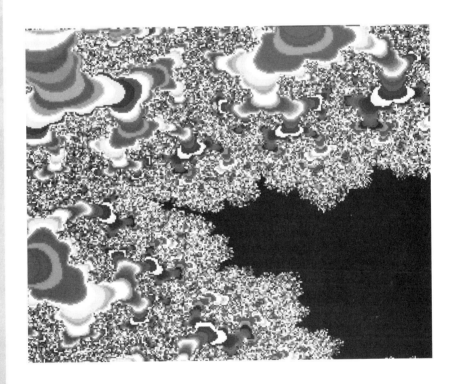

In 1962, Edward Lorenz was attempting to develop a model of the weather when he observed some strange discrepancies in the behavior of his model [Lorenz93]. Lorenz had simplified his model until it consisted of only three differential equations, which, in addition to being a simplified weather model, also described the flow of fluid in a layer of fluid having a uniform depth and a constant temperature difference between the upper and lower surfaces. Lorenz would start with a known set of initial conditions for *x, y,* and *z,* and add the differentials to the three quantities to come up with a new set of values. Iterating this process would result in a set of values for the three quantities at a later time. This is an ordinary process that is used all of the time in mathematics and physics. Because Lorenz was working with a rather primitive computer and had to share with other users, he wanted to be able to periodically save the values from his computer run so that he could later use these values as the starting point for another run when the computer was again available. But when Lorenz attempted to restart the computer run of the model using the stored values, the results, although apparently starting at the same point where he had recorded the stored data, diverged farther and farther from the previous results as the run continued. Lorenz verified that this was not a computer error but, rather, was caused because he had saved and reentered the data to only three-decimal-place accuracy, whereas the computer data at that point in the original computer run was accurate to six decimal places. This behavior is known as *sensitive dependence on initial conditions.* It has now been found to be characteristic of a number of natural and social systems. Previously, scientists had assumed that systems of equations had an orderly behavior in which a set of approximate initial conditions gave approximate solutions, then when the values of the initial conditions were improved, the results became more accurate. Now we know that in some cases, a slight change in initial conditions doesn't improve the accuracy of results; instead, it causes them to diverge to a totally different path. This is bad news for scientists because a very small change in initial conditions can result in major changes in the results and we never know which set of initial conditions gives us the result we want.

The equations used by Lorenz are the following:

$$dx/dt = 10(y - x) \tag{3.1}$$

$$dy/dt = xz + 28x - y \tag{3.2}$$

$$dz/dt = xy - (8/3)z \tag{3.3}$$

When Lorenz laboriously calculated a number of values for these equations on a primitive computer, he discovered the first of the strange attractors and created the foundation for the discipline of "Chaos," which is creating drastic changes in all fields of science and for which the principle drawing tools are fractals.

STRANGE ATTRACTORS

What is a strange attractor? To answer this question, we must first plot a candidate set of equations in phase space—a space of enough dimensions to permit representing each solution of the equation set at a given time as a single point. For the Lorenz equations just given, a three-dimensional phase space is needed. If the solution to this set of equations were constant throughout time, it would converge in phase space to a single point, the attractor, no matter what the initial conditions had been. If the solution converged to a periodic function, which repeated over and over after a fixed interval of time, the result in phase space would be some form of closed curve, the periodic attractor or limit cycle. If neither of these cases is true, yet the equation has a fully determined path through phase space, which never recurs, the resulting curve is called a *strange attractor*. Whatever set of initial conditions you use, continued iteration will cause the solution to converge to a particular curve or family of curves.

THE LORENZ ATTRACTOR

It's time to take a close look at the Lorenz attractor. The Fractal program uses a technique called Runge-Kutta integration to determine a large number of values along the path that the equations follow in time. The values found are three dimensional; because our display only shows two dimensions, the program allows you to view an isometric projection and also the projection of the curve on any two of the three planes of the three dimensional space. Plate 1 of the color insert shows an isometric projection of this curve. Note, however, that without most of the traditional cues that help our senses to convert a two-dimensional drawing to three dimensions, it is not too easy to understand the exact dimensional qualities of the Lorenz attractor, no matter what kind of projection we use. The color in the color scheme changes each time the value of the x coordinate crosses zero. The curves represent 4,000 iterations of the equation with a time step of 0.01. Unfortunately, the resolution of the display screen has proven inadequate to the task of separating out adjacent portions of the curve. However, no matter how good the resolution of your display, the curves will exceed the resolution capability if enough iterations are run. Using the Fractal program, if you select *Lorenz Attractor* from the *Select Fractal Type* menu, you can then look at the isometric projection shown in the plate and also at projections on any two of the three planes in the three-dimensional system.

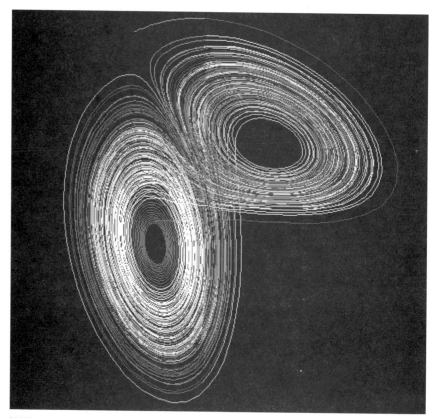

PLATE 1   Lorenz curve isometric projection.

These curves are a sort of encapsulation of what this new science of Chaos is all about, both in its good and its bad features. You would need to watch the curve being drawn and understand that although the curve seems to intersect with itself in the projections, it never does touch itself in actual three-dimensional space.

The good aspect of Chaos is that this simple set of equations can completely describe a very rich and complex nonperiodic behavior. Before investigating this kind of equation system with modern high-speed computers, scientists postulated that such complex behavior must be the result of very complex systems of equations containing many parameters and variables, with possibly a number of random variables thrown in. Now it is known that complex behavior may often be represented in a very simple manner. The bad aspect can be discovered in the following manner: select a starting point somewhere on the very crowded part of the curve; attempt to trace the path from there on.

We already pointed out that the display has inadequate resolution, so that a couple of different portions of the curve double up at the most crowded places. Thus, you can't be sure that you are tracing the right path—as the adjacent curves begin to diverge, your selected path will break in two and you can't be sure which path to follow. How does this apply in the real case? There is no overlapping on the infinite resolution display; each set of initial values determines one and only one path to be followed. But there are an infinite number of paths near the starting point you selected, and which one will be followed depends on how precisely you specified your initial coordinates.

If you selected $x = 3.15678$, for example, you would travel a very different path than if you had selected $x = 3.15679$. And you must remember that $x = 3.15678$ is actually $x = 3.15678000 \ldots$, so that by adding another decimal place with a value other than zero, you can always diverge to a different path altogether. This means that no matter how accurately you select the initial coordinates, if they are *at all* different from the real values that might exist for a natural phenomena, the value that you predict will diverge farther and farther from the *real* value as time progresses. This is bad news for those such as weather forecasters who wish to measure some initial conditions and use them to predict long-term results. Note that measuring more precisely, to come closer to the correct long-term values, does not work because the amount of divergence is not a function of the size of the error, but can differ widely and unpredictably.

RUNGE-KUTTA INTEGRATION

To solve the system of differential equations given earlier, we must use some numerical technique that comes up with an accurate value for x, y, and z as we integrate over time. We have chosen a time step of 0.01. Lorenz, in his original paper, used a double approximation integration technique. However, with more sophisticated computers at our disposal, we can use a more complicated integration method to produce greater accuracy. The method that is used in the Fractal program is the fourth-order Runge-Kutta technique. This method is a one-step procedure that uses only first-order derivatives to achieve the same accuracy obtainable with an equivalent order Taylor expansion using higher order derivatives. Many different sets of coefficients can be used with the Runge-Kutta integration method; the coefficients that we have selected were chosen to minimize the computer time required for each iteration. Given a differential equation

$$dy/dt = f(t,y) \tag{3.4}$$

once the initial condition is established, at each time step, we have

$$y_{n+1} = y_n + k_0/6 + k_1/3 + k_2/3 + k_3/6 \qquad (3.5)$$

where

$$k_0 = h f(t_n, y_n) \qquad (3.6)$$

$$k_1 = h f(t_n + h/2, y_n + k_0/2) \qquad (3.7)$$

$$k_2 = h f(t_n + h/2, y_n + k_1/2) \qquad (3.8)$$

$$k_3 = h f(t_n + h, y_n + k_2) \qquad (3.9)$$

and h is the time step (0.01). Our Fractal program performs 16,000 iterations to produce the desired display.

VIEWING THE LORENZ ATTRACTOR

We have already indicated that our Fractal program will show you an isometric projection of the Lorenz attractor and projections on each set of two of the three planes that make up the three-dimensional space in which the Lorenz Attractor exists. You can also make one final choice, namely selecting *Comparison* under the *Lorenz Attractor* item. For this option, the background is set to white, the drawing color is initially set to black, and the number of iterations is set to 2500. The program is set up to produce two complete passes. On the first, the initial 1200 iterations are just the same as for the XZ projection except that the drawing color remains black. At this point, the current values of x, y, and z are truncated to three decimal places and stored. The program then continues to the end with a new green drawing color. The x, y, and z values used to continue from 1200 iterations are the original values, not the truncated ones. On the second pass, everything is just the same for the first 1200 iterations, and the same black color is used. The result for that part of the curve is just the same as for the first pass. At this point, the truncated values of x, y, and z are substituted for the untruncated values, the color is changed to red, and the process is completed to the end of the 2500 iterations. The resulting curves are shown in Plate 2. The effect noted by Lorenz is fairly obvious in this plate. Changes in the variable values of smaller than three decimal places cause an increasingly large variation between the red and green curves. This display shows clearly the problem Lorenz encountered when investigating these equations. You should note the considerable divergence between the red and green curves. The important thing to think about as you look at these curves is that if you are trying to use this type of equation to predict the future, it just can't be done because we just can't measure the initial conditions accurately enough to know which path we are actually on. However, there are many physical situations in which we are much more interested in the actual shape of the phenomena than of the value at a particular point. For these, the equations work just fine.

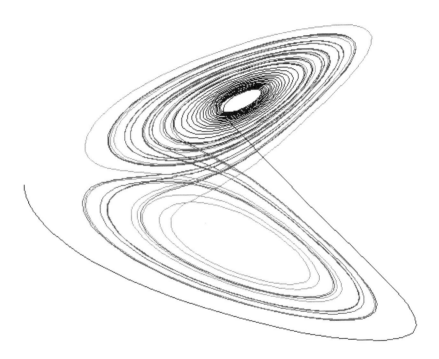

PLATE 2   Comparison of Lorenz curve paths.

OTHER STRANGE ATTRACTORS

The Lorenz attractor proceeds in an orderly fashion from one point to the next as time increases, so that we can draw a good picture of it by drawing lines that connect each pair of adjacent points. Now let's consider a different kind of strange attractor. This one is a dynamical system first reported by Clifford A. Pickover [Pickover90]. It consists of the system of equations:

$$x_{n+1} = \sin(ay_n) - z_n\cos(bx_n) \tag{3.10}$$

$$y_{n+1} = z_n \sin(cx_n) - \cos(dy_n) \qquad (3.11)$$

$$z_{n+1} = \sin(x_n) \qquad (3.12)$$

There is no time step here. Moreover, the point in phase space described by the equations jumps about in what appears to be a totally random fashion. However, when the points for a large number of iterations are plotted, it becomes evident that there is a finite set of positions that the point described by the function can occupy and that the point ultimately goes to this attractor irrespective of the initial conditions. Using the Fractal program, you can create this fractal by selecting the *Strange Attractor* type from the *Select Fractal Type* menu and then selecting which projection you want from the submenu. The resulting displays are shown in Figures 3.1, 3.2, and 3.3 respectively.

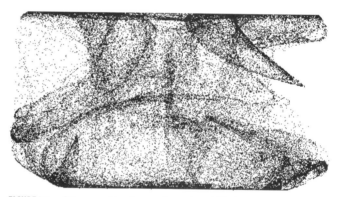

FIGURE 3.1 Strange attractor projected on XZ plane.

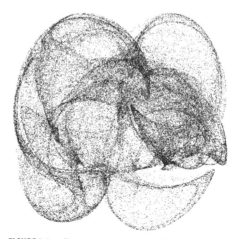

FIGURE 3.2 Strange attractor projected on XY plane.

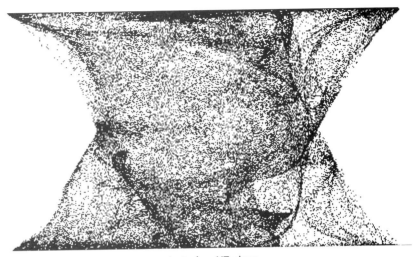

FIGURE 3.3 Strange attractor projected on YZ plane.

REFERENCES

[Lorenz93] Lorenz, Edward N., *The Essence of Chaos*, University of Washington Press, 1993.

[Pickover90] Pickover, Clifford A., *Computers, Pattern, Chaos and Beauty*, St. Martin's, 1990.

WHAT YOU CAN DO WITH L-SYSTEM FRACTALS

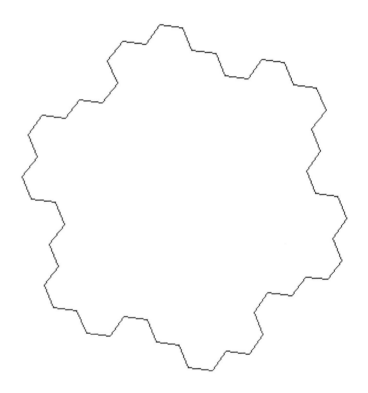

In the next few chapters, we are going to look at some fractals that are called *L-System fractals* because they can be conveniently programmed using a language known as L-Systems that was developed by Aristid Lindenmayer to program models of plants [Prusinkiewicz90]. This language does not have a formal definition, but by using Lindenmayer's concepts and adding a few touches by the author, it was possible to program all the L-System fractals that appear in the Fractal program and in this book. You don't need to worry about the programming details because the parameters for all of these fractals are already set up for you and instructions are also provided so you can create your own fractals using these tools.

HOW L-SYSTEMS WORKS

The L-Systems language makes use of a recursive *initiator/generator* technique that results in complete self-similarity. This technique begins with an initiator, which may be a single line or a simple geometric figure such as a square or hexagon made up of straight line segments. The initiator is defined by a string of characters. Each character has a meaning to the L-Systems subroutines, telling them to turn at the specified angle, generate a line, and so forth. Next, each straight line segment of the initiator is replaced by a generator, which is a pattern of straight line segments that replace the original line segment. The generator is also defined in the L-Systems language by a character string. For each line of the initiator that is replaced, the generator is properly scaled and oriented so that its beginning and end correspond to the beginning and end of the line segment being replaced. At the next iteration, each line segment of the pattern produced by the previous iteration is replaced with the generator pattern, again scaled down and oriented so that the beginning and end of the generator correspond to the beginning and end of the line segment being replaced. This procedure can be repeated as many times as you desire, although after a while your computer display will no longer have enough resolution to display any new detail that you add by repeated iterations. The L-Systems technique is just a language for describing the initiator and generator and their interactions. As with all languages, it is convenient shorthand for describing reality, and it is conveniently manipulated by a computer to create actual fractal drawings. Lindenmayer developed the L-Systems technique while he was a professor at the University of Utrecht. He intended it to be an important tool in generating pictures of plants and trees, but it turns out to have far-reaching capabilities in creating self-similar fractals of many sorts. Please note, however, that there is no established standard for the L-Systems character strings. Those used in the Fractal program, which will be described later in this chapter, although they follow to some extent what others have used, are often designed to make it convenient to create specialized fractals of different kinds. When you're using the *Create L-Systems Curve* capability of the Fractal program, you're pretty much stuck with Fractal characters defined.

THE GEOMETRIC BASIS FOR L-SYSTEMS

The L-Systems language is closely associated with the concept of turtle graphics, which was derived from the Logo computer language. This language was designed to permit untutored persons to draw graphics with a computer. In Logo, graphics are created by a *turtle* that moves about the screen. The turtle can take a step in the direction that it is pointing, in which case a line is usually drawn along the path taken by the turtle. The length of the step is determined by an independent variable. The turtle may also turn. In this case, nothing is drawn; the turtle simply changes its heading so that the next step that it takes will be in a different direction. Originally, the turtle points straight up at the top of the screen. This is the direction *north* on all standard maps, and corresponds to zero degrees. In such a system, the direction angle goes from north clockwise around the face of the compass, with east being 90 degrees, south being 180 degrees, and so forth. This system is great for those familiar with maps, but is less natural to geometricians who would prefer to have the turtle pointing in the *x* direction (toward the right), and having the *x*-axis be zero degrees, with angles measured counterclockwise. There is no official standard defining the initial direction of the turtle or the direction that it turns, so we'll stick with the standard compass and mapping system, with the turtle starting pointed north and angles measured clockwise. Likewise, in defining terms of the L-Systems language, we are not constrained by any official standard. We shall generally try to keep a certain amount of standardization with other versions of the language, but will also feel free to define our own additions to the language where necessary.

SYMBOLS USED IN THE L-SYSTEMS LANGUAGE

Table 4.1 defines the characters used in this version of the L-Systems language and shows which variable contains each string.

Table 4.1 Symbols Used in L-Systems Language

GENERATOR SYMBOL	DESCRIPTION	NO.
d	step without drawing line	1
D	step with line drawn	2
L	left pattern	3
R	right pattern	4
X	X pattern	5
Y	Y pattern	6
T	Pattern with automatically computed orientations	7
B	T pattern with angles reversed	8
t	T pattern reversed back to front	9
b	B pattern reversed back to front	10
H	H pattern	11
P	Random Pattern—randomly select generator 3, 4, or 5	3, 4, 5
p	Random Length—randomly make length 0.75 to 1.25 of nominal	
+	Turn clockwise by designated angle (Angle)	
-	Turn counterclockwise by designated angle (Angle)	
*	Turn clockwise by 2nd designated angle (Angle 2)	
#	Turn counterclockwise by 2nd designated angle (Angle 2)	
[	Store current turtle position and direction	
]	Go back to stored turtle position and direction	
{	Change divisor to 2nd divisor	
}	Change divisor back to original divisor	
(	If level is even, turn clockwise by designated angle; if level is odd turn counterclockwise by designated angle	
)	If level is odd, turn clockwise by designated angle; if level is even turn counterclockwise by designated angle	

OVERVIEW OF THE L-SYSTEMS PROGRAM

Let's look at a simple example of how the L-Systems technique works. We begin with an initiator. Let's say that the initiator is just a straight line, *D*. We have a generator, which is used to replace the line. Suppose that the turn angle is 60 degrees and the divisor 3. The generator is

D–D++D–D. Suppose we want to draw a curve having four levels. For our first pass, which is level four, the string that we implement is just the initiator, which corresponds to a line one step long. Our next pass is level three. Here we replace *D* in the initiator with the generator string. We reduce the step length to one-third of the original, create a line of that length, turn counterclockwise 60 degrees, create another line of step length, turn clockwise 120 degrees, create another line, turn counterclockwise sixty degrees, and create another line. Our geometry and step size has been arranged so that this new pattern of lines ends at exactly the endpoint of the original line from the pass at level four. On the next pass, we go to level two. Every occurrence of *D* in the previous string is replaced by the entire generator string on a reduced scale. When we implement this new string, we find that a smaller replica of the generator pattern replaces each of the four line segments of the previous level. Finally, at level zero, the program actually draws all of the latest collection of lines on the computer display.

MORE COMPLEX GENERATOR SCHEMES

The simple technique just described is adequate for drawing many fractal curves, but sometimes we want to get more complicated. Suppose that we want to have more than one possible generator and switch from one to another under certain circumstances. This is no problem. We simply define several different generators and specify in a generator string which one is to be used for replacement of each line segment. In this program, we have defined generators *D*, *d*, *L*, *R*, *X*, *Y*, and *T*. We've already defined the first two. The next ones, *L* and *R*, somewhat suggest cases where a right and left generator are used, but they really can be used for any purpose, as can *X* and *Y*. The generator *T* is a very special kind of generator. In many complex fractals, we have a generator pattern that we want to use in four different ways. We may want to use it directly to replace a line segment, as we have done above with *D*. However, we may also want to use it in reverse (if it is not symmetrical, starting at the end and drawing the pattern back to the beginning. We call this form of the generator *t*. Both these generators are oriented so that they perform as they should at the top of the line segment being replaced. But we may also want to use mirror images that do the same at the bottom of the line segment. These are called *B* and *b* respectively. (Don't be confused by the small letters. In this case, they mean reversed generators, whereas for *d*, the small letter means that the step is taken without drawing a line. However, this is just the way that each of these generators is defined.) What is unusual about *T* is that after you define it, the program automatically performs the necessary changes to create *t*, *B*, and *b*, so that you then have them available for use in your generator definitions without having to write down whole strings and check to make sure they are correct.

Selecting the level gives you the most control over the appearance that the fractal will have. If you choose level 1, what will be drawn is simply the initiator. If the initiator is a straight line and you select level 2, the picture drawn will be that of the generator. If the initiator is a more complicated geometric figure, level 2 will show the generator replacing each straight line that made up the initiator. As you increase the level of detail, more complex and beautiful curves will appear. Many of the fractals available in the program require only a few levels of detail to produce more complexity than can be shown by the resolution characteristics of the display. However, some L-System fractals require a larger number of levels to show all the detail you may want. For these cases, one of the options of the submenu is *Select Level*. When you click on this, the fractal will be generated at the level shown in the box labeled *Select Fractal Level* at the right-hand side of the display. (The default value in this box is 5.) If you want a different level, you should enter it in this box. (If you make an entry, it must be an integer; anything else will cause the program to crash.) To avoid having the program spend a lot of time trying to work with a level that is too high to obtain useful results, when you run a fractal after selecting *Select Level* from the submenu, each fractal type that uses this feature checks the contents of the *Select Fractal Level* box and reduces it to a defined maximum if it is too high. This value then appears in the *Select Fractal Level* box.

The other main control that you have over the characteristics of L-Systems fractals is the color. You can select the *Select Color Combination* menu and then choose the color that you want for the fractal from the *Image Color* submenu. Independently of image color, you can choose the *Color Background* submenu. From this, you can select one of the predefined background colors, or if you're very particular, you can click on *Select Background Color*. This brings up a display of a number of colors. You can select one, or by clicking on *Define Custom Colors* you can create exactly the color you want. (Note that it's possible to select the same color from the *Image Color* and *Color Background* menus, in which case your display will show nothing.) When you have selected the proper background color, the L-System fractal will be redrawn with the color background you have specified.

Normally, you won't need any size adjustments. All the L-System fractals are designed so that they are centered on the display and fill most of it. However, you may create an L-System fractal at a level where you cannot see all the complexities of the display and you may wonder if the generator patterns were actually drawn as they were supposed to be. The Fractal program allows you to investigate this if you want. At the top of the display are boxes marked *XMax, XMin, YMax,* and *YMin*. For L-Systems fractals, these boxes contain the values 640, 0, 480, and 0 respectively. By changing the values of *XMin* and *Ymin* you can change the starting position of the fractal. By changing the values of *XMax* and *YMax*, you can expand or contract the size of the display. For example if *XMax* – *XMin* is 3 times 640 and *YMax* – *YMin* is 3 times 480, the display will be expanded by a factor of three. You will then only be able to see part of the fractal, but you can create exactly the color you want. When you have selected the proper background color, the L-System fractal will be redrawn with the color background you have specified.

RECURRENCE IN L-SYSTEMS

What happens if we actually carry out the procedure just described with an ordinary program? For the first few levels, there is no problem. With each substitution of the generator for every step in the previous string, the overall string gets longer, but is still manageable. At higher levels, however, this soon gets out of hand. With a relatively simple generator, by the time we get to 16 levels we may need more than 16 megabytes of memory to store the entire string. This quickly taxes the capabilities of a PC. Some L-Systems programs handle this problem by simply quitting when the string gets too large and reporting back, "Not enough memory." We handle the problem with a recursion process that enables us to draw almost any fractal curve, no matter what level is selected. The technique works this way: Instead of actually creating the entire string in advance, each time a step is called for, if the level is zero, we draw a line. But for a higher level, we call a generate program that substitutes the proper generator pattern and reduces the level by one. When the zero level is reached, all the lines are drawn and then the function returns and deals with the next step. In this way, we only deal with a small part of the overall string at any one time, and thus, the whole process becomes manageable.

CREATING L-SYSTEMS FRACTALS

Chapters 5 through 10 introduce you to the characteristics of a number of fractals created by the L-Systems language. You can look at each of these without having to worry about such things as initiators and generators, although each chapter includes the values of these for your reference. Chapter 11 shows you how to create your own L-Systems fractals. After becoming familiar with some of the fractals in Chapters 5 through 10, you should be able to branch out on your own.

REFERENCES

[Prusinkiewicz90] Prusinkiewicz, P., and Lindenmayer, A., *The Algorithmic Beauty of Plants*, Springer-Verlag, 1990.

THE SNOWFLAKE AND OTHER VON KOCH CURVES

The first L-System fractals that we are going to examine are the von Koch fractals [von Koch05]. They belong to a class of fractals called *edge-replacement fractals*. This means that during the iteration process, each edge or line of the current figure is replaced with a pattern of lines called the generator. The von Koch fractals have an additional restriction, namely that the line cannot at any point touch itself. By selecting the *von Koch* item from the *Select Fractal Type* menu, you will be presented with a submenu that allows you to view any of the following types of von Koch fractals: snowflake, complex generator, Gosper, 3-segment, 8-segment, 18-segment, 32-segment, 50-segment, hex-8-segment, Sierpinski triangle, or islands. You can then select the level of the fractal that you want to view, or use the *Select Level* option for fractals where you might want to see higher levels than are allowed by the menu. When you choose this option, the level is shown in a box at the right of the screen labeled *Select Fractal Level*. The default value for this is 5, but you can type in any integer and have the program run at that level. To properly display the fractal at the level you want, you must type in the proper level number before you choose *Select Level*. For each fractal, however, there is a maximum level, after which the resolution of the display is incapable of showing any more detail. If you selected a larger number than this, the computer could spend a lot of time calculating useless detail. To prevent this, if you enter a number that is much too large, the level will be automatically reduced to the maximum specified for that fractal and that number will be displayed in the box. As long as you type in a number, you'll be OK; the program is smart enough so that if you enter a floating-point number it will round it off to the nearest integer before producing the fractal. However, if you enter something ridiculous like "gbv" you will get an error message saying that this isn't a legitimate number.

SNOWFLAKE CURVE

The first curve that we are going to display using the L-Systems technique is the von Koch snowflake, which was first constructed by the mathematician Helge von Koch in 1904. You can display it on your computer by running the Fractals program, choosing *von Koch*, choosing *Snowflake*, and then selecting the level that you want to display. Table 5.1 shows input parameters to L-Systems that are needed to create the snowflake. You don't need to know these to generate the snowflake curves, but if you decide to do some advanced L-Systems research using the information in Chapter 11, you may want to refer back to parameters of one of the specified L-System fractals as a starting point.

Table 5.1 Parameters for the von Koch Snowflake

PARAMETER	VALUE
Initiator	D--D--D
LGenerator[2]	D+D--D+D
Angle	60.0
Divisor	3.0
Start x	170
Start y	330
Start angle	0.0
Line length	300

The initiator, which is shown in Figure 5.1, is an equilateral triangle. It is defined by the string in the initiator, where the angle represented by each minus sign is *angle* (60 degrees) and the line length is 300 pixels.

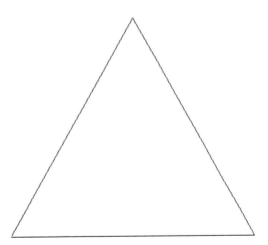

FIGURE 5.1   Snowflake initiator (level 1).

The generator, which is represented by the string in *LGenerator[2]* is shown in Figure 5.2. It divides each line segment into three equal parts. Each segment of the generator has a length that is 1/3 of the length of the line being replaced by the generator (*divisor* = 3.0). The first segment of the generator follows the original line segment. The next two segments form the two sides of an equilateral triangle, the base of which is the second third of the original line. Finally, the fourth segment is identical with the final third of the original line. Thus the number of segments of the generator, N, is four. From Equation 2.1 of Chapter 2, we find the fractal (or similarity) dimension of the snowflake to be

$$D = \log N / \log (1/divisor) = \log 4 / \log 3 = 1.2618 \qquad (5.1)$$

The resulting snowflake for two levels is shown in Figure 5.3, that for three levels in Figure 5.4, that for four levels in Figure 5.5, and that for five levels in Figure 5.6.

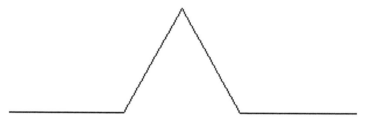

FIGURE 5.2   Snowflake generator.

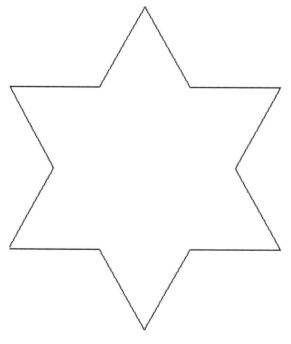

FIGURE 5.3   von Koch snowflake at level 2.

FIGURE 5.4   von Koch snowflake at level 3.

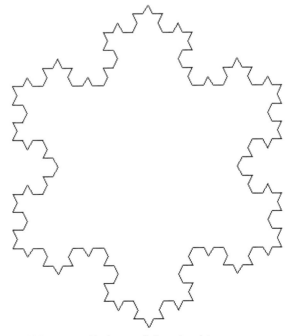

FIGURE 5.5   von Koch snowflake at level 4.

FIGURE 5.6   von Koch snowflake at level 5.

GOSPER CURVE

R. William Gosper discovered this variation of the von Koch curve. The initiator is a regular hexagon, and the generator consists of three segments on a grid of equilateral triangles. Gosper and Martin Gardner called this curve the *flowsnake*, a play on words to indicate that it is very similar in shape to the von Koch snowflake, however in many ways it is completely different [Gardner76]. The Peano-Gosper curve is also often referred to as the *flowsnake*, so we would prefer to avoid this term altogether. Mandelbrot called this curve the *Gosper island* because of its very unusual capability to completely bound the Peano-Gosper curve [Mandelbrot83]. We'll go into this in more detail when we discuss the Peano-Gosper curve. In the meantime, you can look at how these curves fit together by selecting the fractal type *Peano Curves*, then *Peano-Gosper Curve*, then *Peano-Gosper Plus Gosper*, and then looking at the various levels for this pair of curves. We'll call this curve just the *Gosper*. Table 5.2 shows the parameters for this curve.

Table 5.2 Parameters for the Gosper Curve

PARAMETER	VALUE
Initiator	D+D+D+D+D+D
LGenerator[2]	D-D+D#
Angle	60.0
Angle 2	19.1
Divisor	2.645751
Start x	450
Start y	165
Start angle	90.0
Line length	150

Before we get into detail about these parameters, let's look at the initiator for the Gosper curve, which is shown in Figure 5.7 and the generator, which is shown in Figure 5.8. We've drawn the initiator so that two of its sides are vertical lines. Some people prefer to draw it so that two of its sides are horizontal lines. Either way, or any other orientation, is OK; it's a matter of preference. The generator is a little more complicated. The generator for the snowflake was a pattern of four lines, each one-third the length of the line being replaced, and oriented so that the beginning and end points of the generator corresponded to the beginning and end points of the line being replaced. This made replacement a very simple procedure. The generator for the Gosper curve, on the other hand, consists of three line segments, each one-third of the length of the line being replaced, drawn on a grid of equilateral triangles. Note that, as shown, the beginning of the generator corresponds to the beginning point of the line being replaced but that the end of the generator does not correspond to the end point of the line being replaced. Therefore, we need to change the orientation of the generator so it matches the beginning and endpoints of the line being replaced. The first thing we need to consider in using this generator is that its length is not a simple fraction of the original line length, even though the length of each of its segments is such a simple fraction. If you use some simple trigonometry to compute the length of a line connecting the beginning and endpoints of the generator, you will find that the proper scale factor (or *divisor*) is 2.645751, which is where that number comes from in the parameters Table 5.2. Now suppose we go ahead and substitute the generator for each line of the initiator. Because the end of each generator does not correspond to the end of the original line segment, we find that although the basic shape of the curve is unchanged from what it would be for an ordinary generator, the positioning changes significantly, and with each increase of the level used to generate a new version of the curve, the position change becomes more radical. We make the necessary correction as follows: suppose that at the beginning of the generator, instead of having the first segment at a 60-degree angle from the replaced line, we allow it to be at an angle such that the whole generator is tilted until the endpoint corresponds to the endpoint of the line segment being replaced. You can calculate the angle needed to do this yourself, if you want to. It turns out to be 19.1 degrees. We turn the turtle by this angle before we start to draw the generator, and after we are finished, we turn back by the same angle so that the turtle is pointing in the same direction that it would have been for the line that was replaced. Our L-Systems language allows us to do this by letting us define a second angle, *angle2*. We can use * in the generator string to turn forward through this angle and # to turn backward through the same angle. Now, if you run the program for various levels of this fractal, you'll see that the fractal position remains stationary. This gives you some idea of how the Gosper curve is created, but you don't really have to know these details; you can go down through the menu selections to choose the Gosper curve and the program takes care of the rest of the details for you.

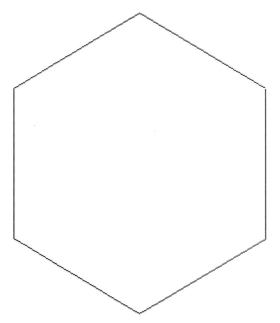

FIGURE 5.7 Initiator for Gosper curve.

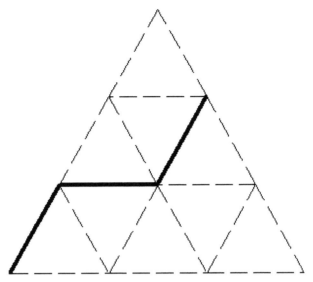

FIGURE 5.8   Generator for Gosper curve.

Applying a little simple geometry shows that if the length from one end of the generator to the other is taken to be 1, the length of each of the three segments is as follows:

$$r = 1/\left(\sqrt{7}\right) \tag{5.2}$$

Because N (the number of segments) is equal to 3, the fractal dimension of the Gosper curve is the following:

$$D = \log 3 /\left(\log \sqrt{7}\right) = 1.1291 \tag{5.3}$$

Figure 5.9 shows the resulting curve for level 2. Figure 5.10 shows the curve for Level 3. Figure 5.11 shows the resulting curve for level 4. Figure 5.12 shows the resulting curve for level 5. Figure 5.13 shows the resulting curve for level 6. You can view these on your computer by selecting the fractal type *von Koch*, then selecting *Gosper* and then selecting the level you want to observe.

The Gosper curve has another very interesting characteristic, namely that of being able to tile a plane. In other words, if identical copies of the Gosper curve at any level are properly positioned, they fit together perfectly. Using eight copies of the Gosper curve for tiling yields the result shown in Figure 5.14 for the sixth level. You can view the tiling at various levels by selecting the fractal type *von Koch*, then *Gosper Tiling*, and then the level you want to look at. The *LGenerator* subroutine that our program uses to generate this type of fractal can only generate one fractal

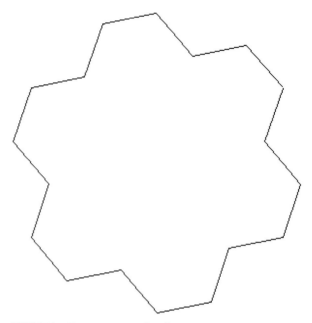

FIGURE 5.9   Gosper curve at level 2.

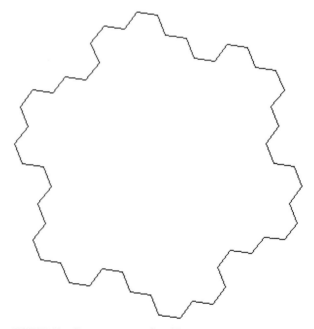

FIGURE 5.10   Gosper curve at level 3.

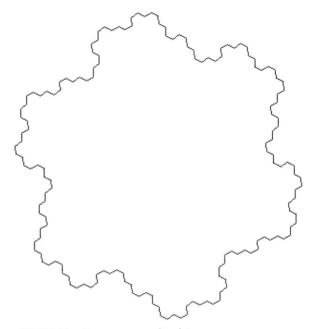

FIGURE 5.11   Gosper curve at level 4.

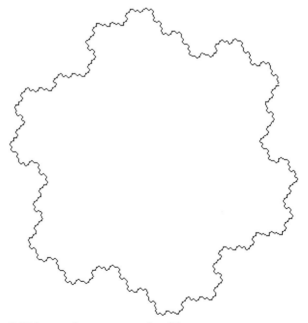

FIGURE 5.12   Gosper curve at level 5.

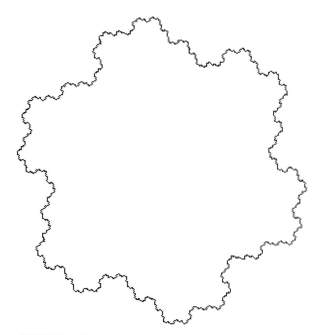

FIGURE 5.13 Gosper curve at Level 6.

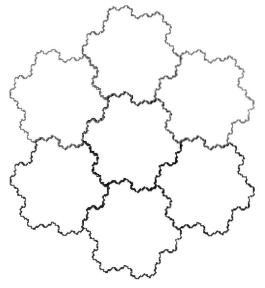

FIGURE 5.14 Sixth-level Gosper curve tiling.

at a time, so to create the picture of tiled fractals that is shown we have to use a different approach. The program calls the subroutine *LGenerator* eight times, to draw eight copies of the Gosper curve. The first time the subroutine works just like it did for the first Gosper curve, first clearing the screen to the background color and then drawing the color specified by *image_color*.

For each additional call to the subroutine, we appropriately change the starting coordinates and prevent clearing the screen so that all the previously drawn Gospers are shown. We also increment *image_color* before each call to the subroutine so that each copy of the Gosper curve is drawn in a different color. The advanced technique that we describe in Chapter 11 for creating your own fractals can't be used in this way, so this is the only place where you can see how tiling is accomplished.

3-Segment Quadric von Koch Curve

This is the first of a series of fractals that are called "quadric" because the initiator is a square and the generator is drawn on a square grid. The first of these curves uses a 3-segment generator. *N* is 3, the same as for the previous curve, but because of the square grid, the geometry is different, giving a segment length of a segment of

$$r = 1\left(\sqrt{5}\right) \tag{5.4}$$

Also, the fractal dimension is different; you will note that it is more space-filling than the Gosper curve:

$$D = \log 3 / \left(\log \sqrt{5}\right) = 1.3652 \tag{5.5}$$

Table 5.3 shows the parameters for the von Koch quadric 3-segment curve. Like the Gosper curve, an adjustment of the angle at the beginning and end of the generator is required to cause the beginning and end-points of the generator to correspond to the beginning and endpoints of the line being replaced.

Table 5.3 Parameters for the von Koch Quadric 3-Segment Curve	
PARAMETER	**VALUE**
Initiator	D+D+D+D
LGenerator[2]	D+D-D#
Angle	90.0
Angle 2	−26.56 →

Divisor	2.2360679
Start x	170
Start y	90
Start angle	0.0
Line length	300

Figure 5.15 shows the initiator and Figure 5.16 shows the generator for the 3-segment quadratic curve. Figure 5.17 shows the curve at level 2. Figure 5.18 shows the curve at level 3. Figure 5.19 shows the curve at level 5. Figure 5.20 shows the curve at level 7. You can use the Fractal program to view these curves on your monitor by selecting the fractal type *von Koch*, then *3 segment*, and finally choosing the level you want to display.

FIGURE 5.15   Initiator for von Koch quadric 3-segment curve.

8-Segment Quadric von Koch Curve

We now come to a fractal whose generator makes use of a square grid and turning angles of 90 degrees. Using this square-grid arrangement, we can create generators so that the beginning of the generator corresponds to the beginning of the line segment being replaced and the end of the generator corresponds to the end point of the line being replaced without any angle adjustments being required. Suppose that the length of each segment of the generator is one-fourth. Then we have

$$r = 1/4 \qquad (5.6)$$

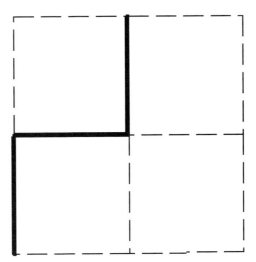

FIGURE 5.16   Generator for von Koch quadric 3-segment curve.

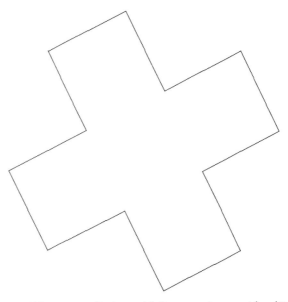

FIGURE 5.17   von Koch quadric 3-segment curve at level 2.

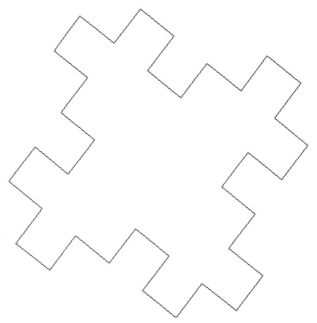

FIGURE 5.18   von Koch quadric 3-segment curve at level 3.

FIGURE 5.19   von Koch quadric 3-segment curve at level 5.

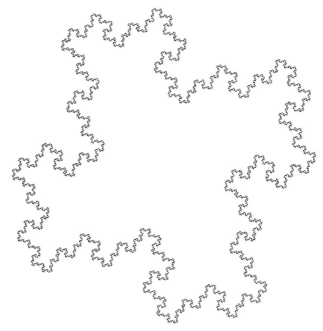

FIGURE 5.20   von Koch quadric 3-segment curve at level 7.

We can draw various generator patterns on the square grid; the only limitation being that we want the curve to have no self-overlap and no self-intersection. If we also want the curve to have the highest fractal dimension possible, we need to find the generator for which N is the largest. Mandelbrot shows mathematically that the highest possible value of N is

$$N_{max} = 1/(2r^2) \qquad (5.7)$$

when r is even and

$$N_{max} = (1 + r^2)/(2r^2) \qquad (5.8)$$

when r is odd. Thus, for $r = 1/4$, we find that N_{max} is 8. For this curve, it is fairly easy to find the pattern that gives maximum N, but as N becomes larger, we will see that considerable trial and error may be needed to determine the best pattern. The fractal dimension of the 8-segment quadric fractal is the following:

$$D = \log 8 \, / \log (1/4) = 1.5 \tag{5.9}$$

Table 5.4 shows the parameters for the von Koch quadric 8-segment curve. The initiator for this curve is the same as that for the 3-segment curve, as shown in Figure 5.15 except that we have chosen to go around the square in the opposite direction. Figure 5.21 shows the generator for this curve. Figure 5.22 shows the curve for level 2. Figure 5.23 shows the curve for level 3. Figure 5.24 shows the curve for level 5. Figure 5.25 shows the curve for level 7. You can use the Fractal program to view these curves on your monitor by selecting the fractal type *von Koch*, then *8 segment*, and finally choosing the level you want to display.

Table 5.4 Parameters for the von Koch Quadric 8-Segment Curve

PARAMETER	VALUE
Initiator	D-D-D-D
LGenerator[2]	D-D+D+DD-D-D+D
Angle	90.0
Divisor	4.0
Start x	210
Start y	350
Start angle	0.0
Line length	220

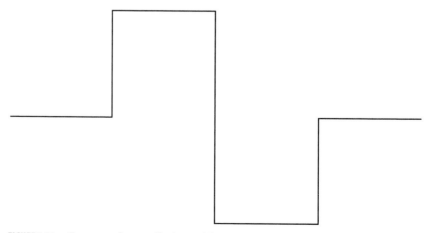

FIGURE 5.21 Generator for von Koch quadric 8-segment curve.

FIGURE 5.22   von Koch quadric 8-segment curve at level 2.

FIGURE 5.23   von Koch quadric 8-segment curve at level 3.

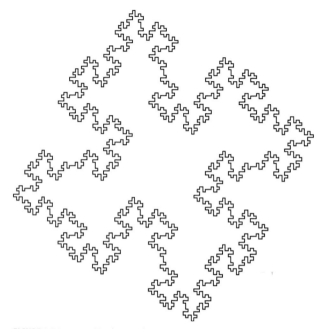

FIGURE 5.24 von Koch quadric 8-segment curve at level 5.

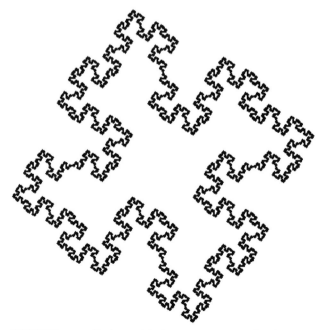

FIGURE 5.25 von Koch quadric 8-segment curve at level 7.

18-SEGMENT QUADRIC VON KOCH CURVE

If we let

$$r = 1/6 \qquad\qquad (5.10)$$

we find that N_{max} is 18. The fractal dimension of this curve is as follows:

$$D = \log 18 \, / \log 6 = 1.6131 \qquad\qquad (5.11)$$

Again, we can create the generator on a square grid. Table 5.5 shows the parameters for the von Koch quadric 18-segment curve.

Table 5.5 Parameters for the von Koch Quadric 18-Segment Curve	
PARAMETER	VALUE
Initiator	D-D-D-D
LGenerator[2]	D+DD-DD-D-D+D+DD-D-D+D+DD+DD-D
Angle	-90.0
Divisor	6.0
Start x	195
Start y	115
Start angle	0.0
Line length	250

The initiator for this curve is the same as that for the 3-segment curve, as shown in Figure 5.15, except that we have chosen to go around the square in the opposite direction. Figure 5.26 shows the generator for this curve. Figure 5.27 shows the curve for level 2. Figure 5.28 shows the curve for level 3. Figure 5.29 shows the curve for level 4. You can use the Fractal program to view these curves on your monitor by selecting the fractal type *von Koch*, then *18 segment*, and finally choosing the level you want to display.

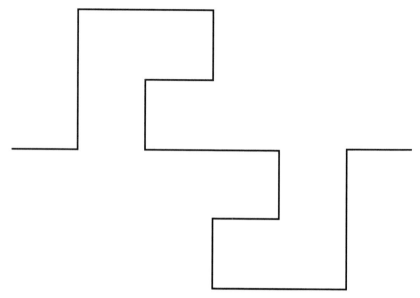

FIGURE 5.26 Generator for von Koch 18-segment curve.

FIGURE 5.27 18-segment quadric von Koch curve at level 2.

FIGURE 5.28   18-segment quadric von Koch curve at level 3.

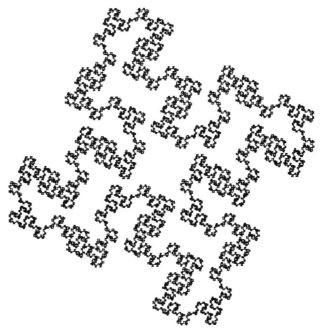

FIGURE 5.29   18-segment quadric von Koch curve at level 4.

32-Segment Quadric von Koch Curve

If we let

$$r = 1/8 \qquad\qquad (5.12)$$

we find that N_{max} is 32. The fractal dimension of this curve is as follows:

$$D = \log 32 \, / \log 8 = 1.6667 \qquad\qquad (5.13)$$

Table 5.6 shows the parameters for the von Koch quadric 32-segment curve.

Table 5.6 Parameters for the von Koch Quadric 32-Segment Curve

PARAMETER	VALUE
Initiator	D+D+D+D
LGenerator[2]	+D-D+D+D-D-DD+D-D-DD-D+D+DD-DD+DD-D-D+DD+D+D-DD+D+D-D-D+D+D-
Angle	90.0
Divisor	8.0
Start x	220
Start y	140
Start angle	0.0
Line length	200

The initiator for this curve is the same as that for the 3-segment curve, as shown in Figure 5.15. Figure 5.30 shows the generator for this curve. Figure 5.31 shows the curve for level 2. Figure 5.32 shows the curve for level 3. Figure 5.33 shows the curve for level 4. You can use the Fractal program to view these curves on your monitor by selecting the fractal type *von Koch*, then *32 segment*, and finally choosing the level you want to display.

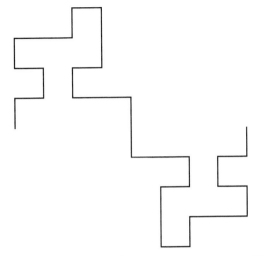

FIGURE 5.30 Generator for 32-segment quadric von Koch curve.

FIGURE 5.31 32-segment quadric von Koch curve at level 2.

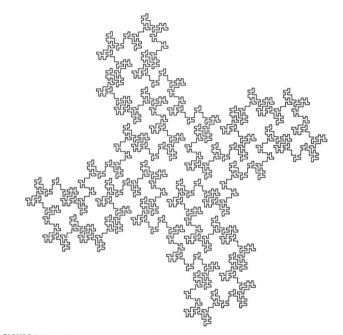

FIGURE 5.32   32-segment quadric von Koch curve at level 3.

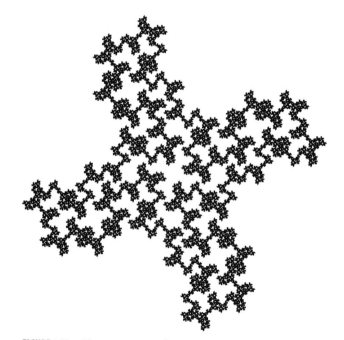

FIGURE 5.33   32-segment quadric von Koch curve at level 4.

50-Segment Quadric von Koch Curve

If we let

$$r = 1/10 \tag{5.14}$$

we find that N_{max} is 50. The fractal dimension of this curve is as follows:

$$D = \log 50 \: / \log 10 = 1.6990 \tag{5.15}$$

As the generator contains more and more segments, it becomes less obvious how the segments are obtained. The process is a sort of trial and error one, but now it is time to develop some guidelines for generator creation. Figure 5.34 shows the generator for the 50-segment curve. The generator grid is also shown. Note that slanting dotted lines have been drawn from the midpoint of one side to the midpoint of the adjacent side (the side that touches the side where the line began).

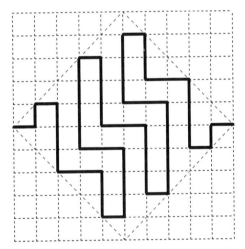

FIGURE 5.34   Generator for 50-segment quadric von Koch curve.

If we are to use the generator to replace line segments that meet at 90-degree angles, we cannot have any part of the generator outside the bounds of the diamond created by these dotted lines. This is sufficient to avoid self-overlapping, but does not prevent self-intersection. To assure against self-intersection, we mentally merge each pair of parallel sides of the diamond. If the generator touches the diamond side at the same point for both sides of a pair, self-intersection will occur. Finally, the easiest way to create the generator is to create it in two parts that are symmetrical (although possibly a mirror image of each other), each beginning at one end of the line segment being replaced and ending at its middle. The constraints are thus

1. Create a half-generator from one end of the line segment to be replaced to its middle, containing $N_{max}/2$ segments.
2. Do not go outside of the diamond.
3. If the generator intersects a point on one of a pair of parallel diamond sides, it may not intersect a corresponding point of the other of the pair of sides.

This is where the trial and error comes in. You need to seek a path that will contain the required number of segments and meet these constraints. Once you have the half-generator created, you can turn the graph upside down and draw the same half-generator to complete the process. Of course, you do not have to go through this process to create any of the 8-segment to 50-segment von Koch curves, because they are already provided for you in the Fractal program. However, if you decide to use the advanced techniques in Chapter 11 to create your own von Koch quadric fractals, you will find these procedures very useful. Table 5.7 shows the parameters for the von Koch quadric 50-segment curve.

Table 5.7 Parameters for the von Koch Quadric 50-Segment Curve

PARAMETER	VALUE
Initiator	D+D+D+D
LGenerator[2]	D-D+D+DDD-DD+DD-D-DDD-DD+DDDD+D+DDD-DD+DDD-D-DDDD-DD+DDD+D+DD-DD+DDD-D-D+D
Angle	90.0
Divisor	10.0
Start x	220
Start y	140
Start angle	0.0
Line length	200

The initiator for the 50-segment von Koch quadric curve is the same as for the 3-segment curve, as shown in Figure 5.15. Figure 5.35 shows the 50-segment curve for level 2. Figure 5.36 shows the 50-segment curve for level 3. Figure 5.37 shows the 50-segment curve for level 4. You can use the Fractal program to view these curves on your monitor by selecting the fractal type *von Koch*, then *50 segment*, and finally choosing the level you want to display. Before we leave the von Koch quadric curves, we should point out that although the fractal dimension increases with the number of segments in the generator, it never reaches 2.0, which is the sign that the entire plane is filled. This is a consequence of the restriction that we placed on von Koch curves that they may never self-intersect.

FIGURE 5.35   50-segment quadric von Koch curve at level 2.

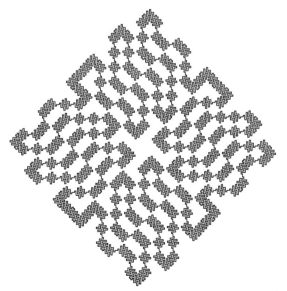

FIGURE 5.36   50-segment quadric von Koch curve at level 3.

FIGURE 5.37   50-segment quadric von Koch curve at level 4.

HEXAGONAL 8-SEGMENT VON KOCH CURVE

All the von Koch curves discussed so far that use the square initiator can easily be adapted to other regular polygon initiators of five or more sides. (The generators have been set up to not be self-overlapping or self-intersecting as long as the sides of the polygon do not intersect at angles of less than 90 degrees. You can experiment with figures other than regular polygons as long as this condition is met.)

Figure 5.38 shows a hexagonal initiator for an 8-segment von Koch curve. The generator is the same as that used for the quadric von Koch 8-segment curve, as shown in Figure 5.21. Table 5.8 shows the parameters for the von Koch hexagonal 8-segment curve.

Table 5.8 Parameters for the von Koch Hex Initiator 8-Segment Curve	
PARAMETER	VALUE
Initiator	D*D*D*D*D*D
LGenerator[2]	D-D+D+DD-D-D+D
Angle	90.0
Divisor	4.0 $\rightarrow$

Start x	230
Start y	80
Start angle	0.0
Line length	180

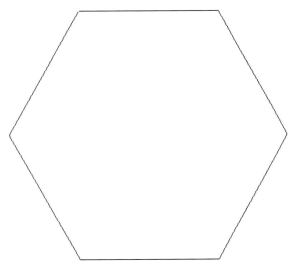

FIGURE 5.38   Initiator for hexagonal von Koch 8-segment curve.

Figure 5.39 shows the curve for level 2. Figure 5.40 shows the curve for level 3. Figure 5.41 shows the curve for level 4. Figure 5.42 shows the curve for level 5. You can use the Fractal program to view these curves on your monitor by selecting the fractal type *von Koch*, then *Hex 8 segment*, and finally choosing the level you want to display.

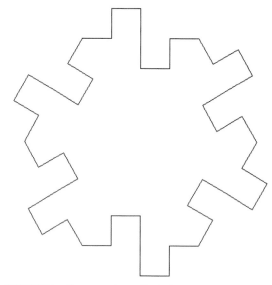

FIGURE 5.39   Hexagonal von Koch 8-segment curve at level 2.

FIGURE 5.40   Hexagonal von Koch 8-segment curve at level 3.

FIGURE 5.41 Hexagonal von Koch 8-segment curve at level 4.

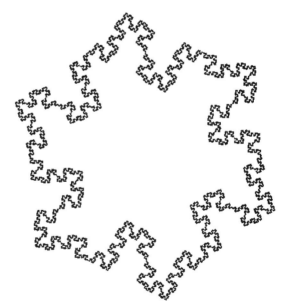

FIGURE 5.42 Hexagonal von Koch 8-segment curve at level 5.

SIERPINSKI TRIANGLE

All the fractals we've looked at so far can be created using only a simple generator. The Sierpinski triangle requires two generators, one specifying that it is to be drawn on the right side of the line segment being replaced and the other to be drawn on the left side [Sierpinski15]. This curve is particularly interesting because there are other ways of creating fractals that are much different from the one we are using here, but for several of them, selecting the right parameters causes a reproduction of the Sierpinski triangle to appear. At this point, mathematically, we don't know what there is about this figure that makes it keep popping up in different fractal creating methods. The initiator for the Sierpinski triangle is a straight horizontal line. Table 5.9 shows the parameters for the von Koch Sierpinski triangle.

Figure 5.43 shows the left (L) generator for the Sierpinski triangle. Figure 5.44 shows the right (R) generator for the Sierpinski triangle. For this curve, N is 3 and r is 1/2 so that the fractal dimension of the curve is as follows:

$$D = \log 3 \,/\, \log 2 = 1.58496 \tag{5.16}$$

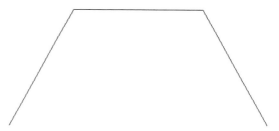

FIGURE 5.43   Left-hand generator for von Koch Sierpinski triangle.

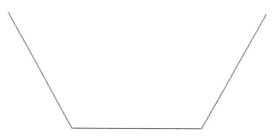

FIGURE 5.44   Right-hand generator for von Koch Sierpinski triangle.

Table 5.9 Parameters for the von Koch Sierpinski Triangle

PARAMETER	VALUE
Initiator	L
LGenerator[3]	+R-L-R+
LGenerator[4]	-L+R+L-
Angle	-60.0
Divisor	2.0
Start x	120
Start y	380
Start angle	0.0
Line length	400

The Sierpinski triangle is one of those fractals for which many levels are needed to give sufficient detail for the curve. To get the necessary flexibility in the program, after you select the fractal type *von Koch* and click on *Sierpinski Triangle*, you have your choice of a few selected lower levels and the option *Select Level*. If you choose this option, the fractal will be computed to the level shown in the *Select Fractal Level* box at the right of the screen. By default, this is set to 5, but you can enter any integer you like. However, if you enter too large a number, it will be reduced to 12 because higher levels than this create details that cannot be resolved on the computer screen. Figure 5.45 shows the Sierpinski triangle at level 6. Figure 5.46 shows the Sierpinski triangle at level 8. Figure 5.47 shows the Sierpinski triangle at level 9. Figure 5.48 shows the Sierpinski triangle at level 12.

You may have noted that the second generator for the Sierpinski triangle is the mirror image of the first and wondered why the automatic features employed for the previous fractal were not used to generate it. It turns out that this is a perfectly good way to generate the fractal and illustrates the simplifications that are possible if we use care in generating our fractal parameters. Table 5.10 shows the parameters for using this alternate method to generate the Sierpinski triangle.

FIGURE 5.45 von Koch Sierpinski triangle at level 6.

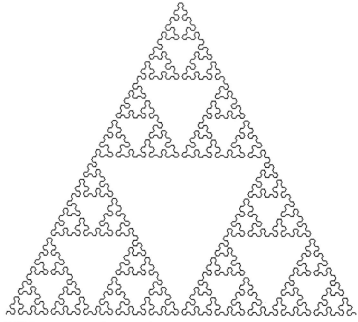

FIGURE 5.46 von Koch Sierpinski triangle at level 8.

FIGURE 5.47   von Koch Sierpinski triangle at level 9.

FIGURE 5.48   von Koch Sierpinski triangle at level 12.

Table 5.10 Alternate Parameters for the von Koch Sierpinski Triangle

PARAMETER	VALUE
Initiator	B
LGenerator[7]	-B+T+B-
Angle	-60.0
Divisor	2.0
Start x	120
Start y	380
Start angle	0.0
Line length	400

ISLANDS CURVE

The islands curve is quite different from the curves that we have looked at previously. It uses as initiator the familiar square that we have seen for all the von Koch quadric curves. However, at higher levels, instead of the generator replacing a line segment, the original line segment is preserved and the generator adds a smaller disconnected rectangle at each side of the original line. Table 5.11 shows the parameters for the von Koch quadric islands curve.

Table 5.11 Parameters for the von Koch Quadric Islands Curve

PARAMETER	VALUE
Initiator	D-D-D-D
LGenerator[1]	dddddd
LGenerator[2]	D-d+DD-D-DD-Dd-DD+d-DD+D+DD+Dd+DDD
Angle	90.0
Divisor	6.0
Start x	210
Start y	350
Start angle	0.0
Line length	220

Figure 5.49 shows the generator for the islands curve. As you will see from Table 5.11, we make repeated use of the parameter d, which causes the turtle to take a step in the direction in which the turtle is pointing, but does not draw a line on the display. In determining the fractal dimension of this curve, you'll see that r is 1/6. Counting the total number of steps that make up the generator, we might assume that N is 22, but not all of these are actually drawn as lines. Eliminating the steps that do not produce a line, we have an N of 18, which seems to be the proper number to use. Thus, we have the fractal dimension of this curve to be the following:

$$D = \log 18 \, / \log 6 = 1.61315 \tag{5.17}$$

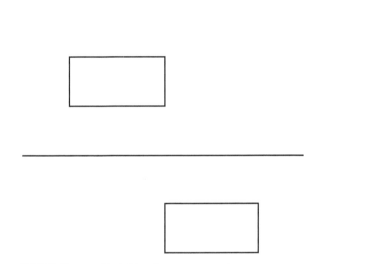

FIGURE 5.49   von Koch islands curve generator.

Figure 5.50 shows the von Koch islands curve at level 2. Figure 5.51 shows the von Koch islands curve at level 3. Figure 5.52 shows the von Koch islands curve at level 4.

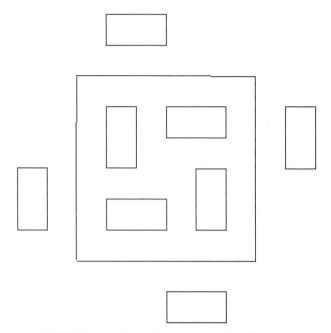

FIGURE 5.50 von Koch islands curve at level 2.

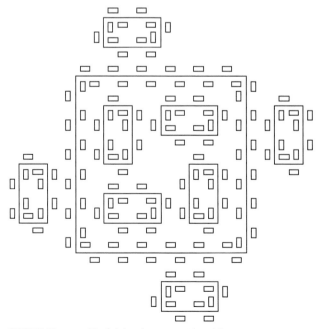

FIGURE 5.51 von Koch islands curve at level 3.

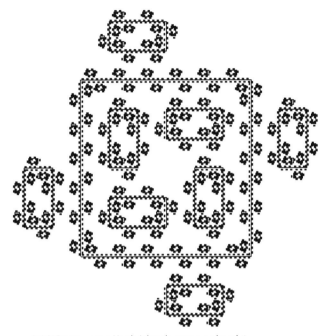

FIGURE 5.52   von Koch islands curve at level 4.

6

PEANO CURVES

C hapter 5 described a number of curves which were characterized by self-similarity, no self-intersection, and no self-overlapping. They had fractal dimensions greater than 1 and less than 2. Thus, no matter how many times the recursion process was applied, the curves would never completely fill the plane. In this chapter, we will consider curves whose fractal dimension, D, is 2. They are called Peano curves because Giuseppe Peano discovered the first of the family, which will be described in the next section, in 1900 [Peano73]. The fractal dimension of 2 has two implications. First, as level approaches infinity, the curves will completely fill the plane. Second, the curves must be self-intersecting—to completely fill the plane, there must be an infinite number of points at which each curve intersects itself.

ORIGINAL PEANO CURVE

Table 6.1 shows the parameters for the original Peano curve. The initiator is simply a horizontal straight line. Figure 6.1 shows the generator for the curve. Because of all of the self-intersections, it is not obvious how the Peano curve is drawn, even if arrows are added to the diagram in an attempt to show the flow. As you look at the diagram, first a step is made up, then a step to the left, then another up, then one to the right, then a step down, then one to the right, then one up, then a step to the left, and finally one up. The generator consists of nine line segments ($N = 9$), each of which has a length of 1/3 of the original line ($r = 1/3$), giving a fractal dimension of

$$D = \log 9 \,/\, \log 3 = 2 \qquad\qquad (6.1)$$

Table 6.1 Parameters for the Original Peano Curve

PARAMETER	VALUE
Initiator	D
LGenerator[2]	D-D+D+D+D-D-D-D+D
Angle	90.0
Divisor	3.0
Start x	320
Start y	90
Start angle	90.0
Line length	300

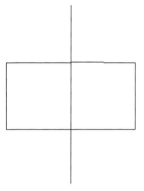

FIGURE 6.1   Generator for original
Peano curve.

Figure 6.2 shows the Peano curve for level 3. Figure 6.3 shows the
Peano curve for level 4. Figure 6.4 shows the Peano curve for level 5. You
can observe this fractal by running the Fractal program, selecting *Peano
Curve* from the *Select Fractal Type* menu, then choosing *Original Peano Curve*
and the desired level from the submenus that appear.

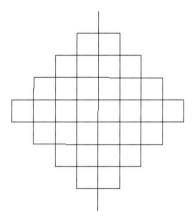

FIGURE 6.2   Original Peano curve at level 3.

One interesting thing about the Peano curve is its application to compression algorithms. One way of saving a photograph in computer memory is to scan the photograph pixel by pixel, saving the color of each pixel
to a different memory location. But this takes a whole lot of memory. A
more efficient way is to provide some elementary coding. For example, as
you scan horizontally across a line of sky, a bunch of pixels may all be of

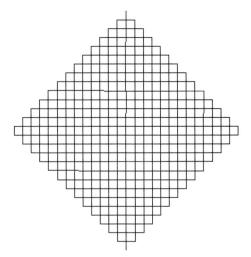

FIGURE 6.3   Original Peano curve at level 4.

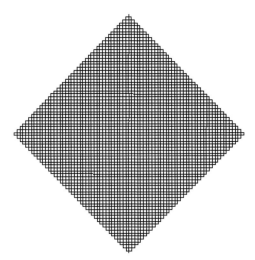

FIGURE 6.4   Original Peano curve at level 5.

the same color. Instead of needing a memory location for each pixel, two memory locations are all that is needed, one for the number of pixels and the other for their color. This works well and greatly reduces the memory needed to store the picture. When you come to the end of the horizontal line and jump to the beginning of the next line, however, it is very un- likely that the ending of one line and the beginning of the next will have the same color. If we scan using the Peano curve pattern, you will note that there are no line ending discontinuities; every pixel is close to the previous one and therefore more likely to be of the same color.

MODIFIED PEANO CURVE

Were it not for the self-intersections of the generator of the original Peano curve, it would be a lot easier to trace the curve and see how it is drawn. We've therefore developed a modification of the Peano curve that rounds off the corners to avoid self-intersection. Table 6.2 shows the parameters for the modified Peano curve. Compare this with the parameters of Table 6.1. You'll see that a generator and associated divisor are the same as those used for the regular Peano curve. These are used for all but the lowest level of the modified curve. Thus, up to that point, there is no difference between the two curves. However, another divisor is only one-sixth of the other divisor and is associated with a generator that has six times as many steps so that the beginning and endpoints are the same. When we come to a *d* designation in this generator, we save the coordinates of the beginning point and then take a step without drawing a line. We then make the specified turn and then come to an *s* designator. This takes another step without drawing a line, but then draws a line from the previously saved set of coordinates to the current position. This results in a diagonal instead of the corner of a square. This divisor and generator is used only at the lowest level of the curve, which is built into the program and therefore cannot be duplicated by the advanced L-Systems techniques of Chapter 4. Figure 6.5 shows the resulting generator for the modified Peano curve, which must be used only at the lowest level of recursion. If this modified generator and divisor were to be used at higher levels, on recursion the program would try to put in numerous extra diagonals in funny places resulting in a very weird curve.

Table 6.2 Parameters for the Modified Peano Curve

PARAMETER	VALUE
Initiator	D
LGenerator[2]	D-D+D+D+D-D-D-D+D
LGenerator[3]	sDDDDd-sDDDDd+sDDDDd+sDDDDd+sDDDDd-sDDDDd-sDDDDd-sDDDDd+sDDDDd
Angle	90.0
Divisor	3.0
Divisor 2	18.0
Start x	320
Start y	90
Start angle	90.0
Line length	300

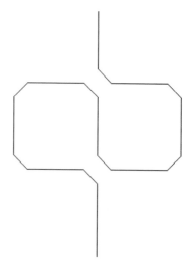

FIGURE 6.5   Generator for modified Peano curve.

The curve is mathematically interesting because it is not quite a true Peano curve. Because the diagonal lines at the corners of the final recursion are a little shorter in length than the length of the two lines that make up a corner in the original Peano curve, the fractal dimension, D, is slightly less than 2. As the number of recursions increases, the fractal dimension changes; as the number of recursions approaches infinity, the fractal dimension approaches 2 as a limit. Figure 6.6 shows the modified

FIGURE 6.6   Modified Peano curve at level 3.

Peano curve at level 3. Figure 6.7 shows the Modified Peano curve at level 4. Figure 6.8 shows the modified Peano curve at level 5.

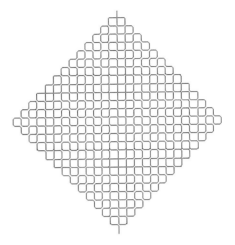

FIGURE 6.7   Modified Peano curve at level 4.

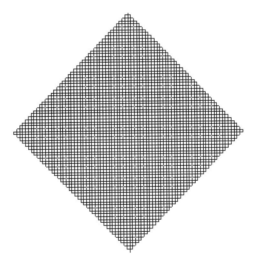

FIGURE 6.8   Modified Peano curve at level 5.

CESARO TRIANGLE

The Cesaro triangle was discovered by the Italian mathematician Ernest Cesaro in 1905 [Cesaro68]. This curve is a little strange for two reasons. First, if a straight line is used as the initiator, the generator is reversed on the first iteration only. One way of coping with this situation is to make use of the *T, t, B,* and *b* set of parameters (where the last three are self-generated). Another is to define two generators using the *R* and *L* parameters. In either of these cases, only one parameter (that of the reversed generator) appears in the definitions because the original generator is only used for the first iteration. Another approach is to define the initiator to include what was the first generator with the two previous methods, rather than as just a straight line. We then need only one generator for the rest of the operations. We only need to use one of these methods in the Fractal program; if you want to try the other techniques using the advanced methods of Chapter 11, the necessary parameters are given.

The second strange thing about this curve is that in creating it, certain lines are completely retraced. Using the first method to create the Cesaro triangle, the initiator is a horizontal straight line. The generator consists of two sides of a right isosceles triangle. Consequently, $N = 2$ and $r = 1\sqrt{2}$. Mathematically, this would make the fractal dimension

$$D = \log 2 / \log\left(\sqrt{2}\right) = 2 \tag{6.2}$$

One might question whether the fractal dimension formula holds true when it includes numerous completely retraced lines. Nobody has shown a mathematical proof for this yet. Maybe you can be the one. The first method of generating the Cesaro curve is using two mirror image generators as we used earlier for the Sierpinski triangle. Table 6.3 shows the parameters for this way of generating the Cesaro triangle.

Table 6.3 Parameters for Two-Generator Cesaro Triangle

PARAMETER	VALUE
Initiator	R
LGenerator[2]	+R--R+
Angle	45.0
Divisor	1.4142135
Start x	170
Start y	325
Start angle	0.0
Line length	300

This version of the Cesaro triangle uses two generators so that it can alternate drawing the generator on one side or the other of the line segment being replaced. These are designated *R* and *L*. Figure 6.9 shows the *R* generator. Figure 6.10 shows the Cesaro triangle at level 3. Figure 6.11

shows the Cesaro triangle at level 4. Figure 6.12 shows the Cesaro triangle at level 8. Figure 6.13 shows the Cesaro triangle at level 14. As the level of iterations approaches infinity, the curve fills a right isosceles triangle.

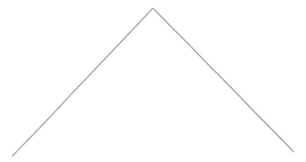

FIGURE 6.9   *R* Generator for Cesaro triangle.

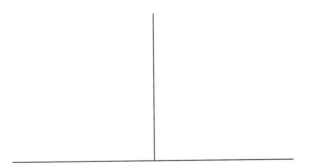

FIGURE 6.10   Cesaro triangle at level 3.

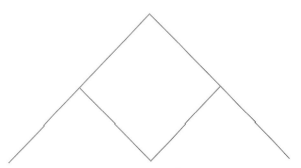

FIGURE 6.11   Cesaro triangle at level 4.

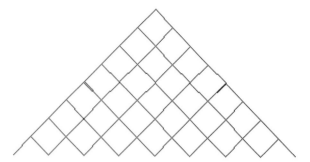

FIGURE 6.12   Cesaro triangle at level 8.

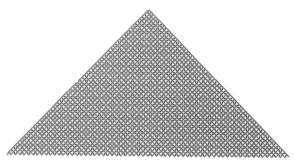

FIGURE 6.13   Cesaro triangle at level 14.

We can also create the two generators (one the mirror image of the other) using the *T, t, B,* and *b* parameters. In this case, the initiator is the same as for the previous method. Table 6.4 shows the parameters for this way of generating the Cesaro triangle.

Table 6.4 Parameters for Cesaro Triangle Using the *T, t, B, b* Method	
PARAMETER	VALUE
Initiator	B
LGenerator[7]	+B--B+
Angle	45.0
Angle 2	45.0
Divisor	1.4142135
Start x	170
Start y	325
Start angle	0.0
Line length	300

Finally, Table 6.5 gives the parameters for creating the Cesaro curve using the first generator of the two previous techniques as the initiator, instead of using a straight line. This only requires a single generator. You'll note that this version requires only half the level value of the previous versions to produce the same picture.

Table 6.5 Parameters for Single Generator Cesaro Curve

PARAMETER	VALUE
Initiator	#D**D#
LGenerator[2]	D+D--D+D
Angle	90.0
Angle 2	45.0
Divisor	2.0
Start x	120
Start y	325
Start angle	0.0
Line length	300

MODIFIED CESARO TRIANGLE

The Cesaro triangle just described is a little hard to trace because the line going out at right angles from the center of the original line segment actually retraces itself, but this is not observable in the drawings. A modification of the Cesaro curve that makes the curve path clearer is possible by changing the angle of the generator from 90 degrees to 85 degrees. Table 6.6 shows the parameters for the modified Cesaro curve. Note that all the parameters are the same as in Table 6.5 except that the angle is changed to 85 degrees and, because this takes away a little of the space for the first and last lines of the generator, the divisor has to be increased to 2.17 to make the beginning and end points of the generator correspond to the beginning and end points of the line being replaced. This makes $N = 4$ and $r = \frac{1}{2.17}$. The fractal dimension is therefore

$$D = \log 4 \, / \log (2.17) \, = 1.7894 \qquad (6.3)$$

Figure 6.14 shows the generator for the modified Cesaro triangle curve. Figure 6.15 shows the modified Cesaro triangle at level 3. Figure 6.16 shows the modified Cesaro triangle at level 4. Figure 6.17 shows the modified Cesaro triangle at level 5. Figure 6.18 shows the modified Cesaro triangle at level 8. Observe the very interesting fractals that are produced by the modification.

Table 6.6 Parameters for Modified Cesaro Curve

PARAMETER	VALUE
Initiator	#D**D#
LGenerator[2]	D+D--D+D
Angle	85.0
Angle 2	45.0
Divisor	2.17
Start x	120
Start y	325
Start angle	0.0
Line length	300

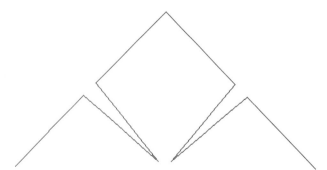

FIGURE 6.14   Generator for modified Cesaro triangle.

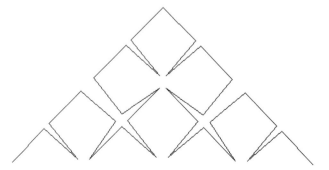

FIGURE 6.15   Modified Cesaro triangle at level 3.

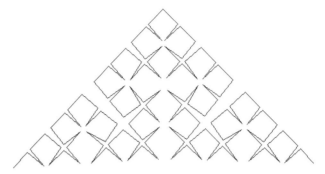

FIGURE 6.16   Modified Cesaro triangle at level 4.

FIGURE 6.17   Modified Cesaro triangle at level 5.

FIGURE 6.18   Modified Cesaro triangle at level 8.

POLYA TRIANGLE

This curve was discovered by George Polya, a professor at Stanford University [Alexanderson99]. The initiator and generator are the same as for the Cesaro curve using a technique that alternates between a generator and its mirror image for each line replaced. The difference from the Cesaro curve is that the generator used to begin the process at each level also alternates. Table 6.7 shows the parameters for generating the Polya triangle. The initiator and generator for the Polya triangle are the same as for the Cesaro triangle as is the technique of alternating from right to left. However, in addition we change the signs of the angles for each level. To do this, we created a new pair of symbols for the L-Systems language, namely the open and close parentheses *( )*. When the program sees these symbols it interprets them as plus and minus angles whose sign is to be changed at each new level. The *(* and *)* signs in the generator strings thus cause a change in the turtle angle the same as the + and − signs, except that instead of always using the default *angle* they use a parameter *angle3* whose sign is set corresponding to the level currently being operated on. This results in a completely different curve from that given by the Cesaro triangle. Figure 6.19 shows the Polya triangle initiator. Figure 6.20 shows the Polya triangle generator. Figure 6.21 shows the Polya triangle at level 4. Figure 6.22 shows the Polya triangle at level 8. Figure 6.23 shows the Polya triangle at level 12.

Table 6.7 Parameters for Polya Triangle	
PARAMETER	**VALUE**
Initiator	R
LGenerator[3]	(L))R(
LGenerator[4]	)L((R)
Angle	45.0
Divisor	1.4142135
Start x	170
Start y	325
Start angle	0.0
Line length	300

FIGURE 6.19   Polya triangle initiator.

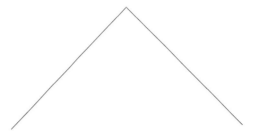

FIGURE 6.20   Polya triangle generator.

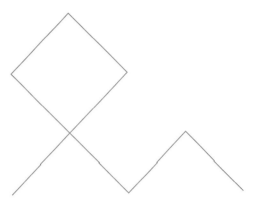

FIGURE 6.21   Polya triangle at level 4.

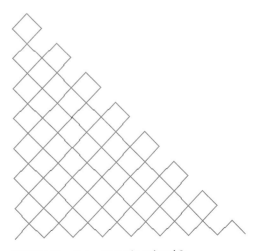

FIGURE 6.22   Polya triangle at level 8.

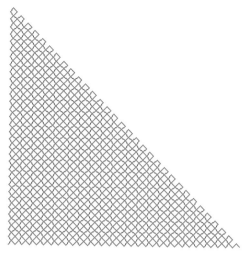

FIGURE 6.23   Polya triangle at level 12.

PEANO-GOSPER CURVE

Figure 6.24 shows the generator for the Peano-Gosper curve and the associated grid of equilateral triangles that defines it. The geometry of the situation can easily be determined from this figure. This curve requires a modifying angle at the beginning and end of the generator to properly line it up with the line being replaced. There are seven line segments ($N=7$), and the length of each one is

$$r = 1/\sqrt{7} \tag{6.4}$$

The fractal dimension is

$$D = \log 7 / \log\left(\sqrt{7}\right) = 2 \tag{6.5}$$

This curve has the interesting characteristic that it just fills the interior of the Gosper curve given in Chapter 5. Table 6.8 shows the parameters for generating the Peano-Gosper curve. You can view this curve on your display by selecting the fractal type *Peano*, choosing *Peano-Gosper*, choosing *Peano Gosper Alone*, and then the level you want to view.

Table 6.8 Parameters for Peano-Gosper Curve	
PARAMETER	VALUE
Initiator	R
LGenerator[3]	*+R-LL--L-R++R+L#

$\rightarrow$

LGenerator[4]	*R-L--L+R++R+l-#
Angle	60.0
Divisor	2.6457513
Start x	190
Start y	315
Start angle	0.0
Line length	260

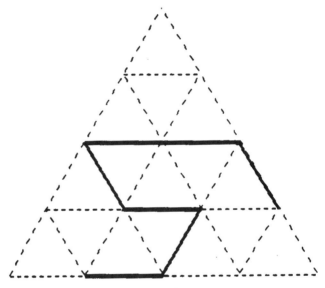

FIGURE 6.24   Generator for Peano-Gosper curve.

Figure 6.25 shows the Peano-Gosper curve at level 3. Figure 6.26 shows the Peano-Gosper curve at level 4. Figure 6.27 shows the Peano-Gosper curve at level 5. Figure 6.28 shows the Peano-Gosper curve at level 6. The program also allows you to superimpose the Peano-Gosper and Gosper curves. You can do this by selecting the fractal type *Peano*, then choosing *Peano-Gosper*, and then choosing *Peano Gosper Plus Gosper*. An example of this combined curve is shown in Figure 6.29, with the Gosper curve shown by a heavier line around the boundary of the figure. The program has to put together two different L-Systems generating cases to make this combined curve, so it cannot be reproduced with the advanced techniques of Chapter 11.

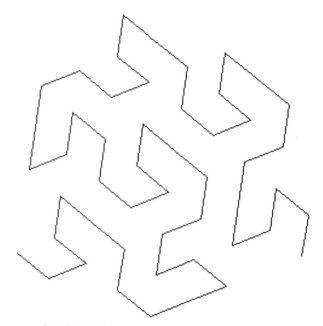

FIGURE 6.25 Peano-Gosper curve at level 3.

FIGURE 6.26 Peano-Gosper curve at level 4.

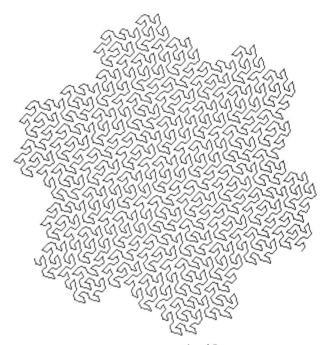

FIGURE 6.27   Peano-Gosper curve at level 5.

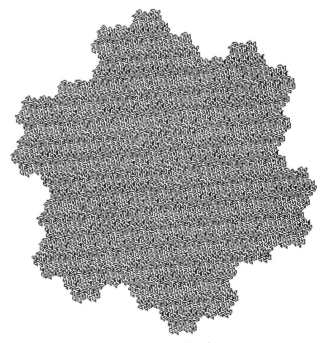

FIGURE 6.28   Peano-Gosper curve at level 6.

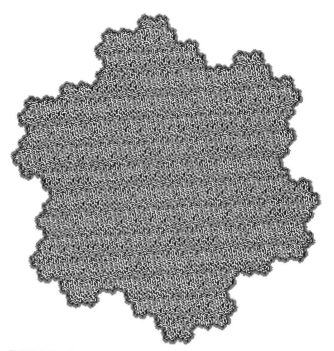

FIGURE 6.29   Peano-Gosper and Gosper curves combined at level 6.

HARTER-HEIGHWAY DRAGON CURVE

You may remember that one of the ways of creating the Cesaro curve was to use two generators. Interestingly enough, if we change the initiator from *R* to *L* and interchange the two generators, a completely different curve is created. This is known as the Harter-Heighway dragon curve (because it looks somewhat like a dragon). This curve was first investigated by physicists John Heighway, Bruce Banks, and William Harter [Davis70]. Its fractal dimension is 2, making it one of the class of Peano curves. Table 6.9 shows the parameters for the Harter-Heighway dragon.

Table 6.9 Parameters for Harter-Heighway Dragon Curve	
PARAMETER	VALUE
Initiator	L
LGenerator[3]	+L--R+
LGenerator[4]	-L++R-
Angle	45.0
Divisor	1.414120
	→

Start x	200
Start y	200
Start angle	0.0
Line length	300

Heighway developed a method for creating this curve by properly folding a piece of paper, but the development of fast home computers has obsoleted the paper-folding method. Figure 6.30 shows the Harter-Heighway dragon curve at level 3. Figure 6.31 shows the Harter-Heighway dragon curve at level 4. Figure 6.32 shows the Harter-Heighway dragon curve at level 5. Figure 6.33 shows the Harter-Heighway dragon

FIGURE 6.30   Harter-Heighway dragon curve at level 3.

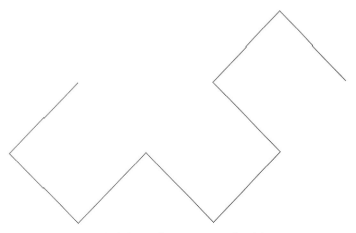

FIGURE 6.31   Harter-Heighway dragon curve at level 4.

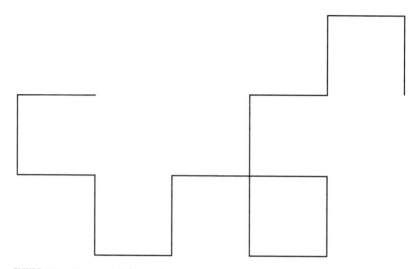

FIGURE 6.32   Harter-Heighway dragon curve at level 5.

FIGURE 6.33   Harter-Heighway dragon curve at level 8.

FIGURE 6.34   Harter-Heighway dragon curve at level 18.

curve at level 8. Figure 6.34 shows the Harter-Heighway dragon curve at level 18.

REFERENCES

[Alexanderson99] Alexanderson, Gerald L., *The Random Walks of George Polya*, Mathematical Association of America, 1999.

[Cesaro68] Cesaro, Ernesto, *Opere scelte / a cura dell'Unione Matematica Italiana e co contributo del Consiglio nazionale delle ricerche*, Edizioni Cremonese, 1968.

[Davis70] Davis, C., Knuth, D. E., "Numerical Representations of Dragon Curves." *Journal of Recreational Math* (April 1970): Vol. 3, No. 2, pp. 66–81.

[Peano73] *Selected Works of Giuseppe Peano* University of Toronto Press, 1973.

Generators with Different Sized Line Segments

All the fractals that we have looked at so far have been created by using generators that have all lines of the same length. We can create fractals of much more beauty and complexity by not imposing this restriction. The L-Systems language handles this by using the symbols { and }. The string representing a fractal by implication uses the *divide* parameter to determine the length of each step defined by the string. However, when { is encountered, a second divider (defined by div2) is used, thereby changing the line length for all succeeding steps until } is encountered, whereupon the program returns to the original line length. Of course, for the fractals already defined in the Fractal program, you don't need to worry about this because it's all internal to the program. However, if you're using the advanced techniques of Chapter 11, you can experiment with different line lengths in your generator by blocking off the steps that are to be of a different line length with the curly brackets as indicated and then inserting the proper value for the *2nd divisor*. Figure 7.1 shows a part of a generator. The first five and last two heavy regular length lines make up this generator. What is missing is whatever must be used to get from the end of the first five lines to the beginning of the next to last line. We're going to look at three different ways of making this transition and will note that each has a significant effect on the fractal dimension and on the resulting fractal picture.

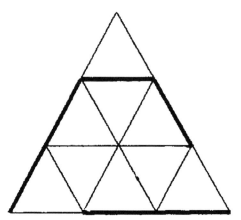

FIGURE 7.1   Partial fractal generator pattern.

PEANO 7-SEGMENT SNOWFLAKE

The simplest way of completing the partial generator shown is to simply draw a straight line connecting the end of the fifth line to the beginning of the next to last line. This fractal was discovered by Mandelbrot, who called it the 7-segment snowflake. Figure 7.2 shows the generator for this curve. To determine the fractal dimension of a fractal that includes two different lengths of line segments, we need to use a different formula than that we used before, namely

$$Nr_1^D + Mr_2^D = 1 \qquad (7.1)$$

where N is the number of line segments of the original length, r_1 is the fraction of new line segments to the original line length (the one being replaced), M is the number of line segments of the second length, and r_2 is the fraction of the second line length to the original line length. For the generator of Figure 7.2, we can compute the fractal dimension by solving the equation:

$$6(1/3)^D + \left(\sqrt{3/3}\right)^D = 1 \qquad (7.2)$$

which gives a fractal dimension of

$$D = 2 \qquad (7.3)$$

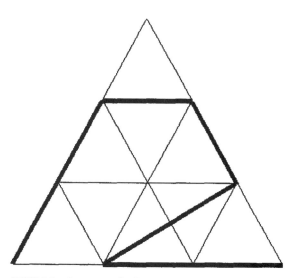

FIGURE 7.2   Generator for Peano 7-segment snowflake curve.

Consequently, this curve is classified as one of the space-filling Peano curves. Table 7.1 shows the parameters for the 7-segment Peano snowflake curve. Figure 7.3 shows the 7-segment Peano Snowflake curve at level 3. Figure 7.4 shows the 7-segment Peano snowflake curve at level 4. Figure 7.5 shows the 7-segment Peano snowflake curve at level 5. Figure 7.6 shows the 7-segment Peano snowflake curve at level 6.

Table 7.1 Parameters for Peano 7-Segment Snowflake Curve

PARAMETER	VALUE
Initiator	T
LGenerator[7]	--Bt++t++t+++{b}-----Bt
Angle	30.0
Divisor	0.577350
Start x	190
Start y	315
Start angle	0.0
Line length	300

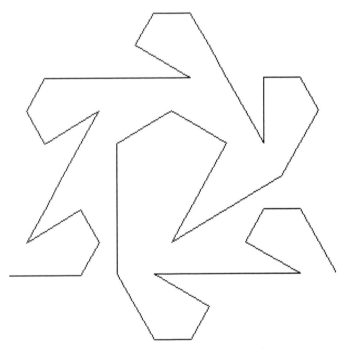

FIGURE 7.3   Peano 7-segment snowflake curve at level 3.

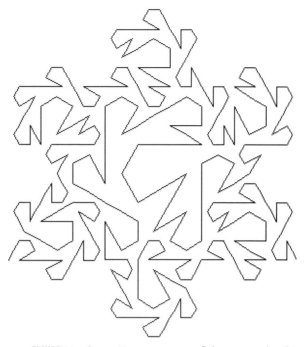

FIGURE 7.4 Peano 7-segment snowflake curve at level 4.

FIGURE 7.5 Peano 7-segment snowflake curve at level 5.

FIGURE 7.6   Peano 7-segment snowflake curve at level 6.

PEANO 13-SEGMENT SNOWFLAKE

We've just seen what happens when we replace the missing part of our partial generator with a single line. Now we're going to try another approach. Instead of a single line, we're going to insert a properly scaled and directed replica of the first five lines of the partial generator. Figure 7.7 shows the resulting generator for the Peano 13-segment snowflake curve. Mandelbrot also discovered it. Again, we use Equation 7.1 to determine the fractal dimension of this curve:

$$7(1/3)^D + 6(1/(3\sqrt{3}))^D = 1 \tag{7.4}$$

which gives a fractal dimension of

$$D = 2 \tag{7.5}$$

Table 7.2 shows the parameters for the 13-segment Peano snowflake curve. For this curve also, there are four choices of generator position, which must be carefully selected for each level and each line segment to ensure that the curve is not self-intersecting or self-overlapping. Figure

7.8 shows the 13-segment Peano Snowflake curve at level 3. Figure 7.9 shows the 13-segment Peano snowflake curve at level 4. Figure 7.10 shows the 13-segment Peano snowflake curve at level 5.

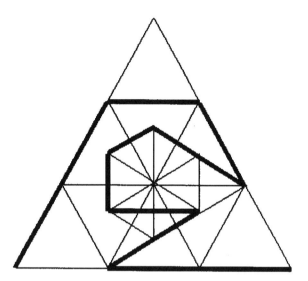

FIGURE 7.7   Generator for Peano 13-segment snowflake curve.

Table 7.2 Parameters for Peano 7-Segment Snowflake Curve	
PARAMETER	**VALUE**
Initiator	T
LGenerator[7]	--BT++T++T+++++{TB--B--B---}+++++TB}
	-----BT
Angle	30.0
Divisor	3.0
Second divisor	1.732051
Start x	190
Start y	315
Start angle	0.0
Line length	300

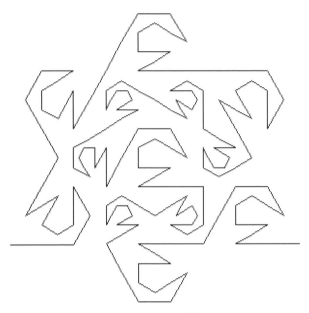

FIGURE 7.8   13-segment Peano snowflake curve at level 3.

FIGURE 7.9   13-segment Peano snowflake curve at level 4.

FIGURE 7.10   13-segment Peano snowflake curve at level 5.

VON KOCH CURVE USING COMPLEX GENERATOR

Now we are going to look at another way of filling in the missing part of our partial generator. This technique uses five smaller lines to complete the generator as shown in Figure 7.11. This generator was also discovered by Mandelbrot. Again, we use Equation 7.1 to determine the fractal dimension of this curve:

$$6(1/3)^D + 5(1/(3\%3)^D = 1 \tag{7.6}$$

which gives a fractal dimension of

$$D = 1.868719 \tag{7.7}$$

Table 7.3 shows the parameters for the 13-segment Peano snowflake curve. For this curve, there are four choices of generator position that must be carefully selected for each level and each line segment to ensure that the curve is not self-intersecting or self-overlapping. We don't need to worry about this, however, because the program takes care of it automatically. We have to thank Mandelbrot for discovering the proper variation to use at each position in the first few levels. If we want to take things farther, we can branch off when we do our own investigations. Figure 7.12 is the von Koch curve using the complex generator at the third level. Figure 7.13 shows the curve for the fourth level. Mandelbrot calls this the monkey tree. Figure 7.14 shows the curve for the fifth level. Mandelbrot calls this split snowflake halls. Figure 7.15 shows the curve for the sixth level.

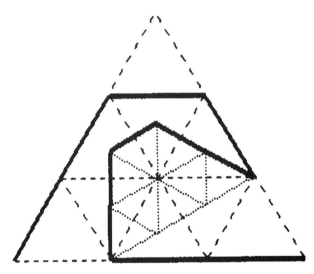

FIGURE 7.11 A complex generator for the von Koch Curve.

Table 7.3 Parameters for the von Koch Curve Using the Complex Generator

PARAMETER	VALUE
Initiator	T
LGenerator[2]	--Bt++T++t+++++{tB--b--bT}---bT
Angle	30.0
Divisor	3.0
Second divisor	1.732051
Start x	190
Start y	315
Start angle	0.0
Line length	300

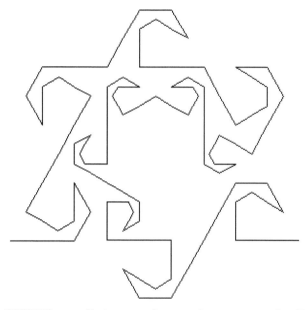

FIGURE 7.12   von Koch curve using complex generator at level 3.

FIGURE 7.13   von Koch curve using complex generator at level 4 (monkey tree).

FIGURE 7.14 von Koch curve using complex generator at level 5 (split snowflake halls).

FIGURE 7.15 von Koch Curve using complex generator at level 6.

FRACTAL DIMENSIONS

In working with the fractals shown in previous chapters of this book, we have become used to the idea that adding more line segments to a generator causes the fractal dimension to increase. The examples given in this chapter show that this isn't true for fractals whose generator consists of line segments of different sizes. Our first example had only 7 line segments, yet it had a fractal dimension of 2. The next example had 13 line segments, and it had a fractal dimension of 2. So, for many more line segments, the fractal dimension didn't change. Well, maybe we hit some sort of limit. But our third example had 11 line segments, and its fractal dimension, of 1.868719, was smaller than the fractal dimension of the other two examples, one of which had fewer line segments and the other of which had more line segments. There seems to be no logical mathematical explanation for this. If you can come up with one, you might go down in history. At any rate, you should use caution in drawing conclusions about the fractal dimension when designing your own fractals.

THE HILBERT CURVE

he Hilbert curve is one of the Peano family of curves, but it has some subtle differences. So far, all the L-Systems fractal curves we've encountered are what are known as *edge-replacement* fractals. In other words, take an initiator and replace every edge in its pattern with a new pattern of lines known as a generator. Then we replace each edge of this new figure with the generator pattern at a reduced scale to get the next iteration. We may do this as many times as we desire. Or at least for as long as our display device is capable of depicting the resolution of each new figure. The Hilbert curve, however, is one of a class of curves for which this technique does not apply. To generate the Hilbert curve, we must instead use a technique called *node-replacement*. The node-replacement technique works by designating two generators, r and l, which are inserted at designated junctions between lines (nodes) for levels above 0 but are not used at level 0. The initiator for the Hilbert curve is a straight line. David Hilbert [Hilbert27] discovered the Hilbert curve. Table 8.1 shows the parameters for the Hilbert curve.

Table 8.1 Parameters for Hilbert Curve

PARAMETER	VALUE
Initiator	L
LGenerator[2]	D
LGenerator[3]	+rD-lDl-Dr+
LGenerator[4]	-lD+rDr+Dl-
Angle	90.0
Divisor	3.0
Start x	160
Start y	380
Start angle	-90.0
Line length	900

Let's see how this works. For level 2, the initiator is replaced by the left generator, which is +rD–lDl–Dr+. When we print this, the rs and ls do nothing so what we actually draw is +D–D–D+. Figure 8.1 shows the resulting fractal at level 2. For level 3, we insert the proper r or l generator in place of each occurrence in the level 2 pattern. The result is +-lD+rDr+Dl- D–+rD–lDl–Dr+D+rD–lDl–Dr+–D–lD+rDr+Dl–+. When we drop out the rs and ls and canceling angles we end up with D+D+D–DD–D–D+D+D–D–DD–D+D+D. Figure 8.2 shows the resulting fractal at level 3.

FIGURE 8.1   Hilbert curve at level 2.

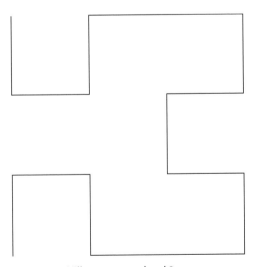

FIGURE 8.2   Hilbert curve at level 3.

The fractal dimension of the Hilbert curve is not obvious. We may approach it in this way, which you can check in the figures. Assuming for the moment an initial divisor of 2, the divisor at level n is 2_n and the number of line segments is $2^{2n} - 1$. This gives a fractal dimension of

$$D = log(2^{2n} - 1)/log(2^n) \qquad (8.1)$$

The limit of this expression as n approaches infinity is 2.0, indicating that the Hilbert curve is one of the class of space-filling curves.

One nice thing about the edge-replacement technique is that each line at the current level is replaced by a generator pattern that is scaled down so that it begins and ends at the beginning and endpoints of the line being replaced. Thus, the size of the fractal that is drawn is essentially the same, regardless of the *level* selected. This is not true when node replacement is used. New generator patterns are placed between existing lines, so the fractal keeps growing, although the amount of growth decreases as line segments become shorter and shorter. One approach is just to ignore this phenomena. Just start with a size that is small enough so that even the highest level you are concerned with will produce a fractal that fits onto the display screen. Unfortunately, this may result in some low-level fractals being too small for satisfactory observation. However, if you are generating your own fractals using the techniques described in Chapter 11, you must use this approach. Another technique, which is used here, is to pick a different divisor for each fractal level, with the divisor chosen by trial and error so that every level of the fractal is essentially the same size. This gives a nice display at each level, but this method does not lend itself to a simple calculation of fractal dimension. These divisors are built into the Fractal program, so they are a part of the Hilbert curve generating software that you don't have access to. Figure 8.3 shows the Hilbert curve at level 4. Figure 8.4 shows the Hilbert curve at level 5. Figure 8.5 shows the Hilbert curve at level 6. Figure 8.6 shows the Hilbert curve at level 7.

FIGURE 8.3   Hilbert curve at level 4.

FIGURE 8.4   Hilbert curve at level 5.

FIGURE 8.5   Hilbert curve at level 6.

FIGURE 8.6   Hilbert curve at level 7.

HILBERT II CURVE

Table 8.2 shows the parameters for a different kind of Hilbert curve known as the Hilbert II curve. Except for the definition of the generators and the divisors, this is very similar to the original Hilbert curve and uses the same node-replacement technique. Figure 8.7 shows the Hilbert II curve at level 2. Figure 8.8 shows the Hilbert II curve at level 3. Figure 8.9 shows the Hilbert II curve at level 4. Figure 8.10 shows the Hilbert II curve at level 5.

Table 8.2 Parameters for Hilbert II Curve

PARAMETER	VALUE
Initiator	L
LGenerator[2]	D
LGenerator[3]	1DrD1+D+rD1Dr-D-1DrD1
LGenerator[4]	rD1Dr-D-1DrD1+D+rD1Dr
Angle	90.0
Divisor	3.0
Start x	160
Start y	380
Start angle	-90.0
Line length	300

FIGURE 8.7   Hilbert II curve at level 2.

FIGURE 8.8   Hilbert II curve at level 3.

FIGURE 8.9 Hilbert II curve at level 4.

FIGURE 8.10 Hilbert II curve at level 5.

USING THE HILBERT CURVE FOR DISPLAY DATA STORAGE

Suppose we have a graphic whose color data is represented by a three-dimensional volume in which the *x* and *y* dimensions are the same as they were for the display, but the third dimension represents color. We would like to record this as a long string in a single file. One way to do this is to scan through each plane, line by line. But when we move from one line to the next, any continuity of color data that might let us reduce the size of the file by setting codes for a number of adjacent pixels of the same color is lost. What we need is a way of scanning through the three-dimensional space that will give us a one-dimensional result in which points that were close together in the original space will still be close together on the resulting line. Thus, a block of a single color on the original display will be lumped together on the resulting line and is suitable for compression to a few bytes.

The Hilbert curve performs exactly this function. It scans an n-dimensional surface and reduces it to a one-dimensional line, and it has the characteristic that points that are close together on the n-dimensional surface are close together on the resulting line. There is some loss of information on the closeness of points because a single dimension cannot possibly have the same degree of spatial associativity that can be achieved with a higher dimension of space. However, this loss is minimal compared with other techniques that might be used for transforming the data. F. H. Preston, A. F. Lehar, and R. J. Stevens of the S. R. D. B. Home Office in England have developed algorithms for using the Hilbert curve to map image data and for compressing the resulting information. They call the Hilbert curve a *Peano curve*, but what they are using is the Hilbert curve described in this chapter.

REFERENCES

[Hilbert27] Hilbert, David, "The Foundations of Mathematics," in *The Emergence of Logical Empiricism*, Garland Publishing, Inc., 1996. (Article originally published in 1927.)

FASS Curves

A whole class of curves are called FASS curves because they are space-*F*illing, self-*A*voiding, *S*imple, and self-*S*imilar. These curves are similar to the von Koch quadric curves, except that the initiator is always a straight line. The angle for these curves is limited to 90 degrees. As you will see when we show some examples of these curves, the number of orientations of the generator is limited, enabling us to get more line segments into a generator. If we do this properly, we can achieve a fractal dimension of 2.0. This implies that the curve will eventually fill a whole section of a plane, as *limit* approaches infinity. An interesting fact about FASS curves is that they can be either of the edge-replacement type or of the node-replacement type. If you're thinking of creating your own FASS curves using the advanced techniques of Chapter 11, you'll find it fairly easy to create edge-replacement types, but it takes a lot of ingenuity to figure out the generators that are needed to create node-replacement FASS fractals.

FASS 1 CURVE

Table 9.1 shows the parameters for the first FASS curve.

Table 9.1 Parameters for FASS Curve 1	
PARAMETER	VALUE
Initiator	L
LGenerator[3]	LL-R-R+L+L-R-RL+R+LLR-L+R+LL+R-LR-R-L+L+RR-
LGenerator[4]	+LL-R-R+L+LR+L-RR-L-R+LRR-L-RL+L+R-R-L+L+RR
Angle	90.0
Divisor	5.0
Start x	160
Start y	390
Start angle	0.0
Line length	300

You'll note that there are two generators used for this curve, the left (L) generator and the right (R) generator. Unlike other times that we've used these two generators, however, they are not mirror images of each other. Looking at the images, you'll note that they have the same general shape but one is reversed and mirrored to obtain the other. Figure 9.1

shows the left generator and Figure 9.2 the right generator. Figure 9.3 is the FASS 1 curve at level 3 and Figure 9.4 is the FASS 1 curve at level 4.

FIGURE 9.1   Left generator for FASS 1 curve.

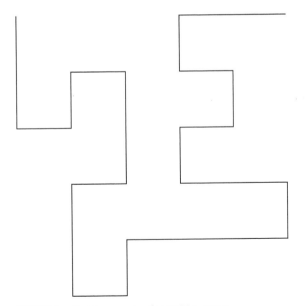

FIGURE 9.2   Right generator for FASS 1 curve.

FIGURE 9.3 FASS 1 curve at level 3.

FIGURE 9.4 FASS 1 curve at level 4.

FASS 2 CURVE

Table 9.2 shows the parameters for the second FASS curve.

Table 9.2 Parameters for FASS Curve 2

PARAMETER	VALUE
Initiator	T
LGenerator[7]	bbb+TT+T+b-T-bb-Tb+T-b-bTb+TTT+bb+T+T-b-bT-b+TTT+bb+T+T-b-bT-b+TT+b+T-b-bb-TTT
Angle	90.0
Divisor	7.0
Start x	190
Start y	315
Start angle	0.0
Line length	300

This curve uses the *T* parameter, which causes the program to automatically create generator strings *t*, *B*, and *b*, as described earlier. You'll note, however, that only two of these, generators *T* and *b*, are actually used to create the fractal. Figure 9.5 shows the *T* generator. Figure 9.6 is the FASS 2 curve at level 3.

FIGURE 9.5 *T* Generator for FASS 2 curve.

FIGURE 9.6   FASS 2 curve at level 3.

FASS 3 CURVE

Table 9.3 shows the parameters for the third FASS curve. This curve uses the same technique used for FASS 2, but with a different original (*T*) generator. Figure 9.7 shows the *T* generator. Figure 9.8 is the FASS 3 curve at level 3.

Table 9.3 Parameters for the Third FASS Curve

Table 9.3 Parameters for the Third FASS Curve	
PARAMETER	**VALUE**
Initiator	T
LGenerator[7]	-bb+T+T-b-bT-B+Tb-T+b+T-bTT+b+TbTbT-b+TbTb-T-bbTbT-b+TbT+T+bt-B+TbTbT-b-bTbTbT-b+TT+b+T-bTT+b+Tb-b-T+T+b-b-TT+b+Tb-b-T+T+b-b-TT
Angle	90.0
Divisor	9.0
Start x	190
Start y	315
Start angle	0.0
Line length	300

FIGURE 9.7   *T* generator for FASS 3 curve.

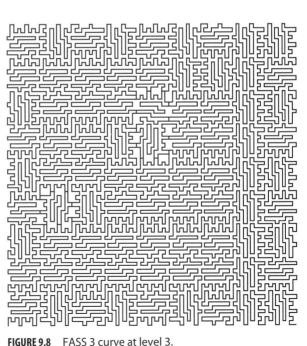

FIGURE 9.8   FASS 3 curve at level 3.

FASS 4 CURVE

The FASS fractals that we have seen so far are all edge-replacement fractals. The next four FASS fractals that we are going to look at are created by the node-replacement technique. Chapter 8 described how this technique works to insert new generator patterns between old lines rather than as replacements for old lines. Using this technique causes the size of the fractal to grow as the level increases, although for each increase in level, the growth factor is smaller. For the Hilbert curves, we built into the program a change in divisor with level so that the size of the fractal on the display appeared to be relatively constant. For the FASS node-replacement fractals, we didn't do this, so you'll notice a distinct change in size. Table 9.4 shows the parameters for the fourth FASS curve. Figure 9.9 shows the generator for the FASS 4 curve. Figure 9.10 is the FASS 4 curve at level 3. Figure 9.11 is the FASS 4 curve at level 4. Figure 9.12 is the FASS 4 curve at level 5.

Table 9.4 Parameters for the Fourth FASS Curve

PARAMETER	VALUE
Initiator	L
LGenerator[1]	D
LGenerator[3]	1D-rDr-Dl+D+1DlDl+DrDr-
LGenerator[4]	+1DlD-rDrDr-D-rD+1Dl+Dr
Angle	90.0
Divisor	3.0
Start x	190
Start y	360
Start angle	0.0
Line length	300

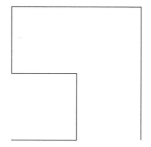

FIGURE 9.9   FASS 4 curve generator.

FIGURE 9.10 FASS 4 curve at level 3.

FIGURE 9.11 FASS 4 curve at level 4.

FIGURE 9.12 FASS 4 curve at level 5.

FASS 5 Curve

Here is another FASS curve that uses the node-replacement technique. As a result of this technique, the size of the fractal increases with level, although each time the level is incremented, the size change becomes smaller until, as the level approaches infinity, there is no discernable change in size. Table 9.5 shows the parameters for the fifth FASS curve. Figure 9.13 shows the generator for the FASS 5 curve. Figure 9.14 is the FASS 5 curve at level 3. Figure 9.15 is the FASS 5 curve at level 4. Figure 9.16 is the FASS 5 curve at level 5. Figure 9.17 is the FASS 5 curve at level 6.

Table 9.5 Parameters for the Fifth FASS Curve

PARAMETER	VALUE
Initiator	-L
LGenerator[1]	D
LGenerator[3]	lDrDl+D+rDlDr-D-lDrDl
LGenerator[4]	rDlDr-D-lDrDl+D+rDlDr
Angle	90.0
Divisor	3.0
Start x	190

$\rightarrow$

Start y	360
Start angle	0.0
Line length	300

FIGURE 9.13   Generator for the FASS 5 curve.

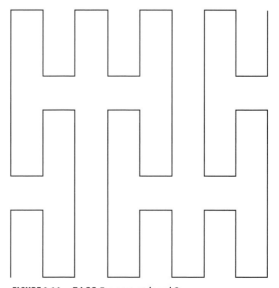

FIGURE 9.14   FASS 5 curve at level 3.

FIGURE 9.15   FASS 5 curve at level 4.

FIGURE 9.16   FASS 5 curve at level 5.

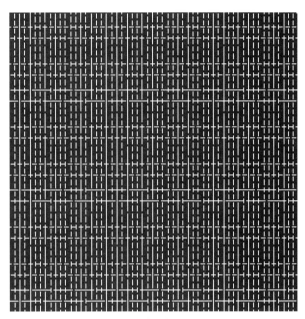

FIGURE 9.17   FASS 5 curve at level 6.

FASS 6 CURVE

This is another FASS curve that uses the node-replacement technique. As a result of this technique, the size of the fractal increases with level, although each time the level is incremented, the size change becomes smaller until, as the level approaches infinity, there is no discernable change in size. Table 9.6 shows the parameters for the sixth FASS curve. Figure 9.18 shows the generator for the FASS 6 curve. Figure 9.19 is the FASS 6 curve at level 3. Figure 9.20 is the FASS 6 curve at level 4. Figure 9.21 is the FASS 5 curve at level 5.

Table 9.6 Parameters for the Sixth FASS Curve

PARAMETER	VALUE
Initiator	L
LGenerator[1]	D
LGenerator[3]	1D1D-rDr-D1D1+DrD+1D1+Dr-D-rD+1D1+DrDrDr-
LGenerator[4]	+1D1D1D-rDr-D1+D+1D-rDr-D1D-rDrD+1D1+DrDr
Angle	90.0 $\rightarrow$

Divisor	4.0
Start x	150
Start y	400
Start angle	0.0
Line length	340

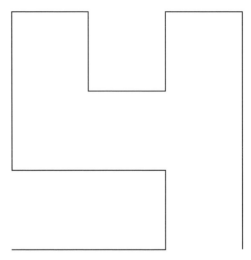

FIGURE 9.18   Generator for FASS 6 curve.

FIGURE 9.19   FASS 6 curve at level 3.

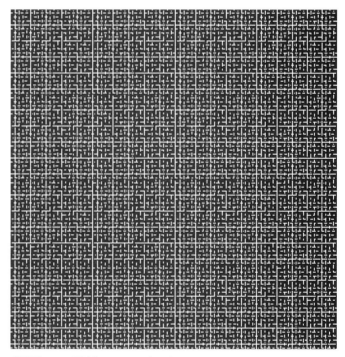

FIGURE 9.20   FASS 6 curve at level 4.

FIGURE 9.21   FASS 6 curve at level 5.

FASS 7 CURVE

The FASS 7 curve also uses the node-replacement technique. As a result of this technique, the size of the fractal increases with level, although each time the level is incremented, the size change becomes smaller until, as the level approaches infinity, there is no discernable change in size. Table 9.7 shows the parameters for the seventh FASS curve. Figure 9.22 shows the generator for the FASS 7 curve. Figure 9.23 is the FASS 7 curve at level 3. Figure 9.24 is the FASS 7 curve at level 4. The FASS 7 curve is rather strange in that it seems to violate the requirement that all FASS curves have 90-degree angles. However, you will note that in the generators, we frequently use the terms l and r, which at the final drawing level do nothing. Eliminating these terms from the generators puts two angle signs together whenever there is an angle, resulting in either 0 degrees or 90 degrees, so that the curve works out OK. Looking at the figures, you can see that this does give curves that are of the FASS nature.

Table 9.7 Parameters for the Seventh FASS Curve

PARAMETER	VALUE
Initiator	L
LGenerator[1]	D
LGenerator[3]	l-D-r+D+l-D-r+D+l+D+r-D-l+D+r+D+l-D-r+D+l+D+r+D+l-D-r-D-l-D-r+D+l-D-r-D-l+D+r-D-l-D-r+D+l-D-r+D+l
LGenerator[4]	r+D+l-D-r+D+l-D-r-D-l+D+r-D-l-D-r+D+l-D-r-D-l-D-r+D+l+D+r+D+l-D-r+D+l+D+r-D-l+D+r+D+l-D-r+D+l-D-r
Angle	45.0
Divisor	5.0
Start x	150
Start y	400
Start angle	0.0
Line length	350

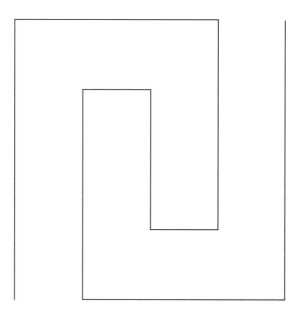

FIGURE 9.22   Generator for FASS 7 curve.

FIGURE 9.23   FASS 7 curve at level 3.

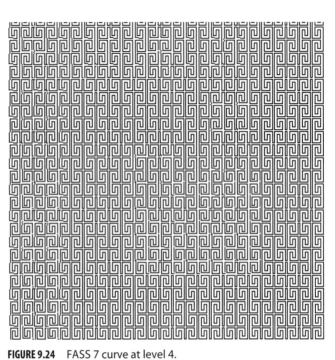

FIGURE 9.24 FASS 7 curve at level 4.

The Fractal program can display all these FASS curves. Simply choose the *Select Fractal Type* menu, select the *FASS Curves* type, and then choose the FASS curve type you want to view from the submenu that appears. Another submenu will then appear that allows you to select the level of the fractal that you want to display.

TREES

The L-Systems generated curves described in the previous chapters have all been characterized by lines that followed each other in order. We previously mentioned, that the L-Systems language was developed by Lindenmayer to describe the geometric structure of trees and plants [Prusinkiewicz90].For such constructions, we need a method to permit branching. To do this, we have included two L-Systems commands represented by square brackets *[]*. When the left-hand square bracket is encountered, the *x* and *y* coordinates of the turtle and the turtle angle are stored in a stack. Processing of the string then continues until the right-hand square bracket is encountered. At this point, the turtle *x* and *y* coordinates and the turtle angle are restored to the values that were stored in the stack at the time the left-hand bracket occurred. By having the next thing that occurs in our string be an angle that is in a different direction than that which we originally traveled from this point, we can have a branching point on a tree limb or trunk. Thus, we process what happens on one branch, and then return to the branching point to process what happens on another branch. The trees that we are going to show in this chapter are called *stick trees* because they are drawn with lines having the thickness of a single pixel. These show clearly the general shape and structure of the tree, but do not take into account its thickness. Nor do we attempt to include the capability for the tree to have buds, flowers, or leaves. Before we start producing these stick trees, let's look at some of the characteristics of real trees.

REAL TREES

Leonardo da Vinci looked at the structure of trees and decided that the tree was actually a pipe system designed to carry nutrients throughout the tree. Therefore, he decided that the sum of the cross-sectional areas of all tree branches at a given height is constant. This should not be too surprising; the tree is required to pass nutrients from the roots to the leaves and for a given nutrient requirement one might expect that the "pipe" cross-sectional area required for nutrient transportation would be constant, regardless of height or the number of pipes. When we translate this observation to diameters (or widths when we make our two-dimensional drawings), we have an expression of the form:

$$D_0^{\alpha} = D_1^{\alpha} + D_2^{\alpha} \qquad (10.1)$$

where D_0 is the diameter of the stem, D_1 and D_2 are the diameters of the two branches that the stem splits into, and α is 2 according to da Vinci. There are other forms of treelike structures. The simple model just given probably applies better to river networks than to trees because the likelihood that more than two tributaries of a river system would join at the same place is remote. Other trees are found in the human body in the form of the arterial blood transportation system and the bronchi. Investigations have shown that a good approximation for α for the bronchial system is 3 and for the arteries is 2.7. However, all this is an oversimplification. All we have to do is look at a straight section of the trunk of a tree where there are no branches and we see that in real life, this trunk section is not of constant diameter, but tapers toward the top. Thus, more is going on than just a simple piping system. Also, our proposed model only allows for a branch to two new arms, where a real tree may have three or more arms at a junction point.

In real life, there are two classes of trees, deciduous (trees whose leaves fall every year) and conifers (evergreens having cones). These two classes of trees are quite different. The conifers tend to have rings of branches at different heights around a central trunk. This defies the binary branching process; consequently, the tree curves that we generate never look like conifers. Secondly, note that deciduous trees, although they are closer in appearance to our model, still are much more complex in their structure. Binary branching is often the rule, but there are exceptions—a stem splits into more than two branches, for example. Furthermore, the lengths of stems before branching occurs differ randomly from the norm, as do the diameters of branches.

The reason for making a point of all this is that we are next going to present some data on expressions for modeling trees, but we want to make sure that these are not taken as representing the way real trees are constructed. In some literature, authors appear to have been overpowered by their ability to express tree structures mathematically, to the point that the model supersedes reality. Remember, the mathematical formulas are a nice way of generating tree curves, but the real tree is much more complex and much more interesting. If you want a real challenge, try to write a tree program that will cover each of the possible situations for a real tree. Another point you might consider here is that a real tree is probably much more of a fractal than our simple model. Thus, there could be simple mathematical expressions that, when iterated, result in very realistic trees.

Our simple model won't consider limb and trunk thickness. We do, however, have to consider the changes in limb length. McMahon studied various typical trees and concluded that a recursive formula for limb length could be written as

$$L_{n+1} = 2^{-3/(2\alpha)} L_n \qquad (10.2)$$

where L_n is the length of the predecessor branch and L_{n+1} is the length of each of the two successor branches after a split occurs.

TREE DRAWING WITH L-SYSTEMS

Table 10.1 shows the parameters for the first tree. LGenerator[5] contains the string for the *X* parameter. It causes drawing of a vertical line, branching to the right and drawing another line, going back to the branch point and drawing another vertical line, then branching to the left and drawing a line and then going back to the second branch point, branching to the right and drawing another line. Figure 10.1 shows the generator for this tree. Figure 10.2 shows the tree at level 4. Figure 10.3 shows the tree at level 5. Figure 10.4 shows the tree at level 9. If you select *Trees* from the *Select Fractal Type* menu, then choose *First Tree*, and finally select the level you desire, you can view this tree on your monitor using the Fractal program.

Table 10.1 Parameters for the First Tree

PARAMETER	VALUE
Initiator	X
LGenerator[2]	DD
LGenerator[5]	D[+X]D[-X]+X
Angle	22.5
Divisor	2.0
Start x	320
Start y	400
Start angle	-90.0
Line length	180

FIGURE 10.1 Generator for the first tree.

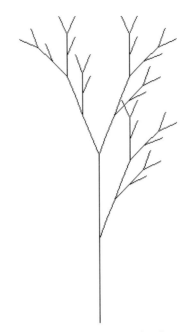

FIGURE 10.2   First tree at level 4.

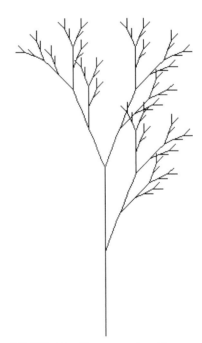

CXFIGURE 10.3   First tree at level 5.

FIGURE 10.4 First tree at level 9.

SECOND TREE

Table 10.2 shows the parameters for the second tree.

Table 10.2 Parameters for the Second Tree

PARAMETER	VALUE
Initiator	D
LGenerator[2]	D[+D]D[-D]D
LGenerator[5]	D[+X]D[-X]+X
Angle	26.5
Divisor	2.7
Start x	320
Start y	440
Start angle	-90.0
Line length	180

One difference between this and the first tree is that the branching angle is 4 degrees larger. Another difference is that at the last branch, after branching to the left, the second tree adds a branch going vertical, whereas the first tree adds a branch going to the right. Figure 10.5 shows

FIGURE 10.5   Generator for the second tree.

FIGURE 10.6   Second tree at level 4.

the generator for the second tree. You can compare it with Figure 10.1 to see the difference from the first tree. Figure 10.6 shows the second tree at level 4. Figure 10.7 shows the second tree at level 5. Figure 10.8 shows the second tree at level 9. As the level increases the seemingly insignificant differences between the two trees result in radically different patterns.

FIGURE 10.7   Second tree at level 5.

FIGURE 10.8   Second tree at level 9.

THIRD TREE

Table 10.3 shows the parameters for the third tree.

Table 10.3 Parameters for the Third Tree	
PARAMETER	**VALUE**
Initiator	X
LGenerator[2]	DD
LGenerator[5]	D[+X][-X]DX
Angle	27.9
Divisor	2.0
Start x	320
Start y	400
Start angle	-90.0
Line length	180

As you will see, the generator for the third tree, shown in Figure 10.9, is completely symmetrical, which results in a set of trees with very pleasing symmetrical properties. Figure 10.10 shows the third tree at level 4. Figure 10.11 shows the third tree at level 5. Figure 10.12 shows the third tree at level 9.

FIGURE 10.9   Generator for the third tree.

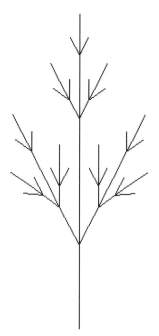

FIGURE 10.10 Third tree at level 4.

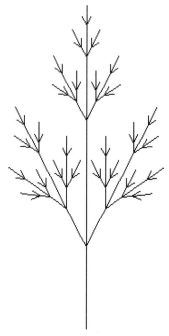

FIGURE 10.11 Third tree at level 5.

FIGURE 10.12   Third tree at level 9.

FOURTH TREE

Table 10.4 shows the parameters for the fourth tree. The fourth tree involves a more complex generator than we've seen before. We use the counterclockwise angle before branching so that everything is tilted toward the left. The minus and plus values of the default angle are then used after branching to create the left and right branches. Each branch has three steps, each having an angle change applied to it. The resulting generator is shown in Figure 10.13. As we go up in level, this gives the effect of a tree that is bent by prevailing winds. Figure 10.14 shows the fourth tree at level 4. Figure 10.15 shows the fourth tree at level 5. Figure 10.16 shows the fourth tree at level 9.

Table 10.4 Parameters for the Fourth Tree

PARAMETER	VALUE
Initiator	D
LGenerator[2]	DD-[-D+D+D]+[+D-D-D]
Angle	23.0
Divisor	2.0 →

Start x	320
Start y	400
Start angle	−90.0
Line length	110

FIGURE 10.13   Generator for the fourth tree.

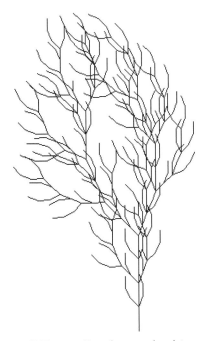

FIGURE 10.14   Fourth tree at level 4.

FIGURE 10.15   Fourth tree at level 5.

FIGURE 10.16   Fourth tree at level 9.

FIFTH TREE

Table 10.5 shows the parameters for the fifth tree.

Table 10.5 Parameters for the Fifth Tree	
PARAMETER	**VALUE**
Initiator	X
LGenerator[2]	DD
LGenerator[5]	D-[[X]+X]+D[+DX]-X
Angle	22.7
Divisor	2.0
Start x	320
Start y	400
Start angle	-90.0
Line length	150

The generator for the fifth tree is shown in Figure 10.17. It is very similar to the generator for the first tree, except that one of the arms of the final branch is twice as long as the other. As you can see by comparing higher levels of the two trees, this small change makes a significant difference in the appearance of the trees. Figure 10.18 shows the fifth tree at level 4. Figure 10.19 shows the fifth tree at level 5. Figure 10.20 shows the fifth tree at level 9.

FIGURE 10.17   Generator for the fifth tree.

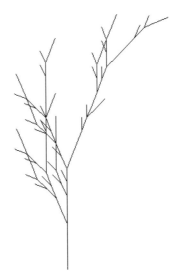

FIGURE 10.18   Fifth tree at level 4.

FIGURE 10.19   Fifth tree at level 5.

FIGURE 10.20   Fifth tree at level 9.

SIXTH TREE

Table 10.6 shows the parameters for the sixth tree.

Table 10.6 Parameters for the Sixth Tree

PARAMETER	VALUE
Initiator	D
LGenerator[2]	D[+D]D[-D][D]
Angle	29.3
Divisor	2.0
Start x	320
Start y	400
Start angle	-90.0
Line length	150

This is another example of how small changes in the angle and generator can dramatically change the characteristics of the tree. Figure 10.21 is the generator for this tree. Figure 10.22 is the sixth tree at level 4. Figure 10.23 is the sixth tree at level 5. Figure 10.24 is the sixth tree at level 7.

FIGURE 10.21   Generator for the sixth tree.

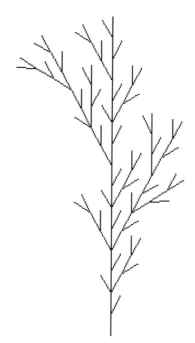

FIGURE 10.22   Sixth tree at level 4.

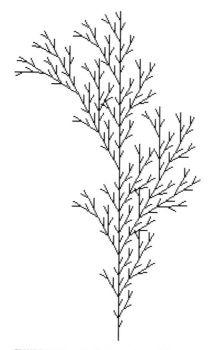

FIGURE 10.23   Sixth tree at level 5.

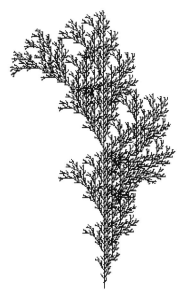

FIGURE 10.24   Sixth tree at level 7.

BUSH

Table 10.7 shows the parameters for the bush.

Table 10.7 Parameters for the Bush

PARAMETER	VALUE
Initiator	RLDDD
LGenerator[2]	D
LGenerator[3]	[-DDD][+DDD]D
LGenerator[4]	[+++X][---X]TR
LGenerator[5]	+Y[-X]L
LGenerator[6]	-X[+Y]L
Angle	18.0
Divisor	1.3
Start x	320
Start y	400
Start angle	-90.0
Line length	60

We call this a bush because the three generators that start at ground level give it a bushlike appearance. Note that six different generators are used to define the characteristics of the bush. The first generator is shown in Figure 10.25. Figure 10.26 shows the bush at level 5. Figure 10.27 shows the bush at level 6. Figure 10.28 shows the bush at level 10.

FIGURE 10.25 First generator for the bush.

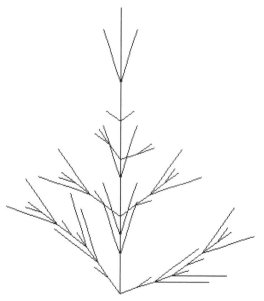

FIGURE 10.26 Bush at level 5.

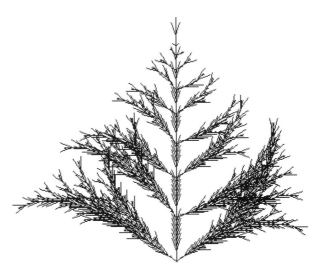

FIGURE 10.27 Bush at level 6.

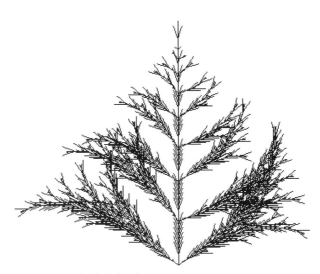

FIGURE 10.28 Bush at level 10.

RANDOMNESS IN TREES

The trees that we have created so far are a little too regular to be representative of trees in nature. Now we are going to introduce a little randomness to increase the reality of our tree images. We can create randomness in trees in two ways. The first is activated by using the parameter p in our fractal defining string. When p occurs, instead of just taking a normal-sized step, the step size is changed from its nominal value. We select a random number from 0 to 1.0 and use it to modify the step size, so that, depending on the number that comes up, the step is somewhere within the limits of 0.75 to 1.25 of the nominal size. This produces what we call a random length tree. The second possibility is to vary the pattern of the generator. To do this, we use the parameter *P*. When *P* occurs in a string, during the iteration process we select a random number between 0 and 1.0; if it is less than 0.333333, we use the generator pattern in LGenerator[3]; if it is between 0.333333 and 0.666667, we use the generator in LGenerator[4]; and if it is between 0.666667 and 1.0, we use the generator pattern in LGenerator[5]. This results in what we call a random pattern tree. If you are using the advanced techniques of Chapter 11, you can introduce randomness into your fractals through these two parameters.

To show how the same basic tree parameters can vary from one iteration to the next when randomness is thrown in, we show three renditions of the same tree on a single display. We do this within the Fractal program by running the same random parameters three separate times with the starting *x* at three different positions to generate three trees side by side. Table 10.8 shows the parameters for a set of random-pattern trees.

Table 8-8 Parameters for Random-Pattern Trees

PARAMETER	VALUE
Initiator	P
LGenerator[3]	P[*P]P[#P]P
LGenerator[4]	P[*P]P
LGenerator[5]	+Y[-X]L
Angle	90.0
Angle 2	26.5
Divisor	1.3
Start y	400
Start angle	−90.0
Line length	140

Note that we don't include *Start x* because it differs for each of the three trees in the display. You can view this fractal at various levels by clicking on *Select Fractal Type,* then *Trees,* then *Random Pattern Tree,* and then on the level you desire. Figure 10.29 is a set of random-pattern trees at level 9.

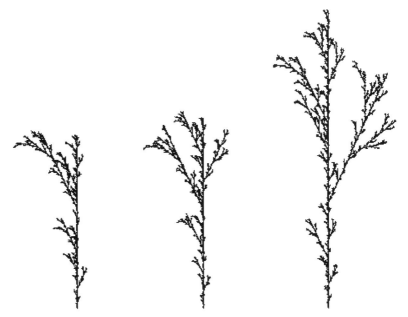

FIGURE 10.29 Random-pattern trees at level 9.

The other way of introducing randomness into trees is by randomly changing the step length. The parameters used for this display are shown in Table 10.9.

Table 10.9 Parameters for Random-Length Trees

PARAMETER	VALUE
Initiator	L
LGenerator[2]	D
LGenerator[3]	[DDp][*Dp]
Angle	90.0
Angle 2	8.0
Divisor	1.4
Start y	440
Start angle	-90.0
Line length	125

Figure 10.30 shows a set of random-length trees at level 9. As you can see, this type of randomness causes the trees to look quite different from the random-pattern trees.

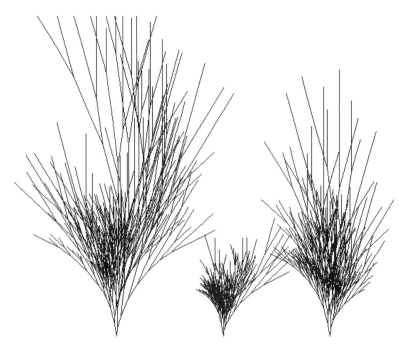

FIGURE 10.30 Typical random-length trees at level 9.

REFERENCES

[Prusinkiewicz90] Prusinkiewicz, P., and Lindenmayer, A., *The Algorithmic Beauty of Plants*, Springer-Verlag, 1990.

11

CREATING YOUR OWN L-SYSTEM FRACTALS

Initiator	
LGenerator[1]	
LGenerator[2]	
LGenerator[3]	
LGenerator[4]	
LGenerator[5]	
LGenerator[6]	
LGenerator[7]	

Angle	0.0	Angle 2	0.0	Start angle	0.0	Line length	
Divisor	1.0	2nd Divisor	1.0	3rd Divisor	1.0
Start X		Start Y		Close

The previous chapters have shown numerous fractals that were created using the L-Systems language. Now you have a chance to create your own L-System fractals. Just click on the menu item *Select Fractal Type* and then on *Create L-Systems Curve*. A menu will appear which allows you to enter the necessary parameters to describe a fractal. You might start by entering the parameters of one of the L-Systems described in the earlier chapters, which you are already familiar with. Once you have entered all the parameters, you can click on *Close* and the fractal will be displayed at the level given in the *Select Fractal Level* box. Once you have inserted a set of parameters, they will stay there for as long as the program is in use or until you decide to change them. Thus, if you want to look at the same fractal at a different level, you insert the desired level in the *Select Fractal Level* box, choose *Create L-Systems Curve* again and then click on *Close*. The same fractal will be displayed at the new level you have chosen without having to reenter the parameters. When you are familiar with this procedure, you are ready to create your own L-System fractals.

CREATING AN INITIATOR AND GENERATOR

To create your own L-Systems fractal, first sketch your desired initiator and generator on a piece of paper. Choose the angle that you will want to use for each turn. (To make greater turns you can use the angle symbol several times.) Now select the character string that will define your initiator. For example, you can define a square by defining your angle as 90 degrees and then defining the string for the initiator as *"D+D+D+D."* You can then define the string for your generator using this same technique but defining a different line pattern. You then put this string into LGenerator[2]. This makes a very simple fractal. For more complex ones, you may need to have several different generators.

USING THE *CREATE L-SYSTEMS CURVE* COMMAND

Figure 11.1 shows the panel that appears when you select the fractal type *Create L-Systems Curve*. Using Table 4.1, you can determine which boxes you should use to insert the strings that you need to create your own fractal and how to make up the strings to perform the actions that you want. In many cases, a number of the LGenerator boxes should remain empty. Strings are given for all the L-System fractals that have been described in the previous chapters, so looking at them should give you a good idea of how to proceed. The *Start angle, Start X,* and *Start Y* boxes allow you to specify the starting angle of the turtle and its starting coordinates on the display. The *Line Length* box determines the size of the fractal. After a trial run, you can reduce this value for a smaller representation of the fractal or increase it for a larger representation. Finally, when you have filled all of the boxes with the values you want, you can click on *Close* and the fractal will be drawn on your display. If you create a fractal that you like, be sure and record the parameters somewhere for future reference before you change them or turn your computer off.

FIGURE 11.1   Panel for creating L-Systems curves.

MORE COMPLICATED FRACTALS WITH L-SYSTEMS

The examples we have given here are relatively simple. Many more complicated fractals can be drawn using the L-Systems technique by using more than one generator or by using branching techniques to create tree-like structures. You've already been exposed to several of these and seen what parameters are required to make them work. If you want to make your own complex fractals, you should have enough tools with the symbols defined to create very elegant and complex fractals. These are limited mainly by your own ingenuity.

12

NEWTON'S METHOD

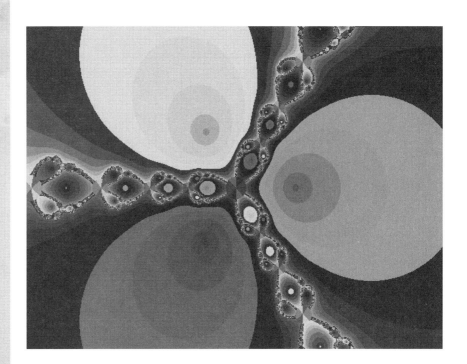

Newton's method is an iterated numerical approximation technique developed by Sir Isaac Newton to obtain the solutions of equations. It is particularly useful for equations that do not have a closed form solution. Consider the following generalized equation:

$$f(z) = 0 \qquad (12.1)$$

We would like to find at least one of the roots of this equation. If the function is fairly simple, there may be a simple mathematical way of obtaining the solution. But what if the function is so complicated or involves such higher powers of the variable that we just don't know how to solve it? Then, we can use Newton's method. This method is based on a truncated Taylor series. Suppose that we first make a guess at the value of a root. Call this guess z_0. It can be shown that if we insert the value z_n into the Taylor series

$$f(z_{n+1}) = f(z_n) + f'(z_n)(z) + (f''(z_n)(\Delta z)^2)/2! + (f'''(z_n)(\Delta z)^3)/3! + \ldots \quad (12.2)$$

the value of Δz that causes the right-hand side of the equation to equal zero, when added to our guess at the root, z_n, gives the exact value of the root. This isn't too practical, however, because taking an infinite number of derivatives is very difficult. Newton, therefore, decided to use only the first two terms of the series, which results in an answer that is not exactly the correct root, but is closer than our original guess. With a little mathematics, we can reframe the two-term equation as follows:

$$z_{n+}1 = z_n - (f(z_n)/(f'(z_n))) \qquad (12.3)$$

where f' is the derivative of f.

Once we obtain a value z_1, which is closer to the actual value of one of the roots than our original guess z_0, we can substitute that value for the z_ns in the equation to obtain a value for z_n, which is closer to the actual root than our previous estimate. This process can be repeated as many times as necessary to obtain the value of the root to any desired accuracy. Next, let's consider how we can use this process to create a fractal. In the *Fractals* program, we are going to work with the equation:

$$z^m - 1 = 0 \qquad (12.4)$$

We let the display space represent the complex plane over the range of values that z may take in our calculations. Then, we let our guess z_0 take on the value represented by each pixel in turn and perform the iteration process until the change in the value of z from one iteration to the next is less than some arbitrary number. We then assume that we have reached the real value of the root and color the pixel according to the number of iterations that were required. The result for a seventh-order equation (m = 7) is shown in Plate 3. (The gradient coloring scheme was used.) When you select *Newton* from the *Select Fractal Type* menu, you will automatically get the default value for a third-order equation. At the right of the display is a box labeled *Newton Exponent.* You can enter any desired value for the exponent and run *Newton* again to obtain a fractal based on the equation having the exponent you entered.

PLATE 3   Seventh-order Newton fractal.

Take a look at Plate 3. There are seven small circles closest to the large red circle in the center. They represent the seven roots associated with the seventh-order equation. When your initial guess for the root (the pixel value) is correct, one iteration will give you the correct result, and the pixel at the center of the appropriate node is colored with the color assigned for one iteration. As the initial guess moves away from this node, the number of iterations needed to obtain the node value increases, and the color changes accordingly. One might think that when the initial guess moves far enough so that it is closer to another node than the one we were looking at, the iterative process will cause the root value to center in on this new node. Actually, the process of changing from one node to another is much more complicated. To show this behavior, the Fractals program includes another color option called Newton. To color the *Newton* fractal using this option, choose the *Select Color Combination* menu and then select *Newton Colors* from that menu. This option only works properly when the Newton exponent is set to 3.0, so be sure that the box labeled *Newton Exponent* contains the default value of 3.0 before you try to use this color combination. What we have done is to define three sets of colors, one having eight shades of red, one having eight shades of blue, and one having eight shades of green. One group is assigned to each root of the equation. To do this, you need some prior knowledge of where the roots are located. For the equation $z^3 - 1 = 0$, it is easy to find the roots because one root is 1. Dividing the equation by $z - 1$ leaves the quadratic equation:

$$z^2 + z + 1 = 0 \qquad (12.5)$$

which can be solved by the quadratic formula

$$z = (-1 \pm (-3)^{1/2})/2 \qquad (12.6)$$

to obtain roots of $-.5 \pm .8660254i$. Knowing that the ultimate value of z will always be one of these three values, we can devise some if tests to determine which color group to use. We then set up the color definitions so that the group that is attracted toward the root 1 is shades of red, the group for $-.5 + .8660254i$ is shades of green, and the group for $-.5 - .86660254i$ is shades of blue. The resulting fractal is shown in Plate 4.

When you look at the resulting fractal, the different shades of a basic color represent the number of iterations that were required for the program to converge to a root. You'll note that there are areas of the program where a very small change in the value of the initial guess causes the end result to move from one root to another, and that the root moved to is not always the one closest to the initial guess. It was once assumed that whatever guess you chose as a starting point, Newton's method would always eventually converge to the nearest root. Plate 4 shows very plainly that this is not true. There are lots of color mixtures and isolated islands of one color within another, which demonstrate that it is quite possible to pick an initial value that converges to a root that is not the nearest to the guessed initial value.

Note that if we take one of the initial guesses that is represented by a tiny point of green, for example, at each iteration of the equation, the result must be on a green area. Otherwise, the result would not be the same root as occurred if this were the starting point rather than a midpoint of the process.

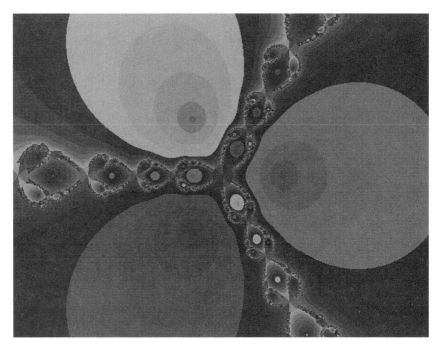

PLATE 4   Third-order Newton fractal colored according to the final root the guess is attracted to.

NONINTEGER EXPONENTS

You do not have to use an integer as the Newton Exponent. If you do use an integer, this integer will also define the number of nodes (corresponding to the number of equation roots) in the fractal picture. If you use a number that is not an integer, the number of nodes will be the same as if you rounded off the exponent, but the fractional part of the exponent causes other interesting color structures within the fractal. The Fractal program is set up so you can enter any floating-point number into the box labeled *Newton Exponent*. Try some for yourself.

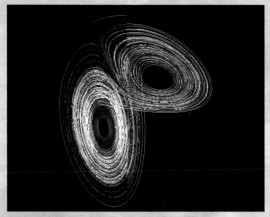

PLATE 1   Lorenz Curve Isometric Projection.

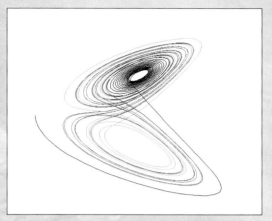

PLATE 2   Comparison of Lorenz Curve Paths.

PLATE 3   Seventh-Order Newton Fractal.

PLATE 4   Third Order Newton Fractal colored according to the Final Root the Guess is Attracted to.

PLATE 5   The Mandelbrot Set

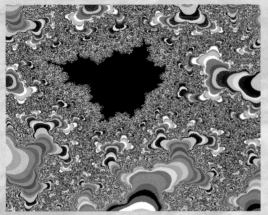

PLATE 6 Expanded Mandelbrot Set Showing Self-Similarity.

PLATE 7 Expanded Mandelbrot Set with Gradient Coloring

PLATE 8 Julia Set 1.

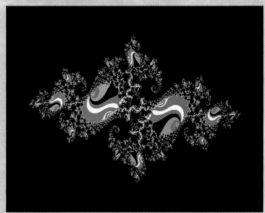

PLATE 9 Julia Set 2.

PLATE 10 Julia Set – Hypnoteyes.

PLATE 11 Self-Squared Dragon.

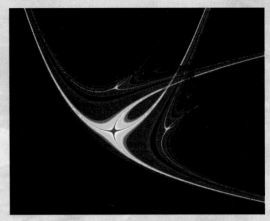

PLATE 12 Pyapunov Swallow.

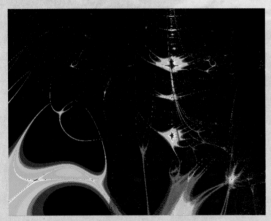

PLATE 13 Lyapunov Zircon Zity.

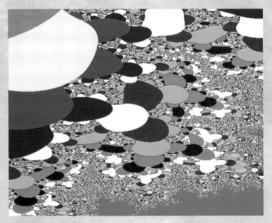

PLATE 14 Expanded Cosine Fractal

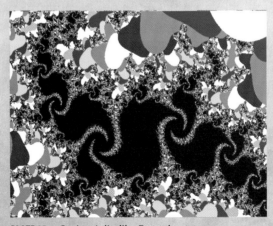

PLATE 15 Cosine Julia-like Fractal.

PLATE 16   Expanded Sine Fractal.

PLATE 17   Sine Julia-like Fractal.

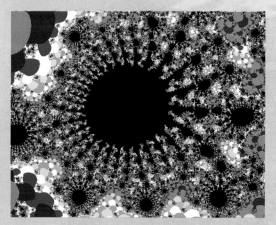

PLATE 18   Hyperbolic Cosine Julia-like Fractal.

PLATE 19   Hyperbolic Sine Julia-like Fractal.

PLATE 20   Exponential Julia-like Fractal.

PLATE 21   Sixth Order Bernoulli Julia-like Fractal.

PLATE 22   Fifth Order Chebyshev C Julia-like Fractal.

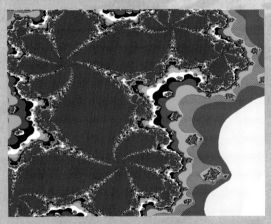

PLATE 23   Sixth Order Chebyshev T Julia-like Fractal.

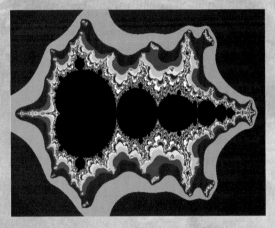

PLATE 24   Legendre Fourth Order Fractal.

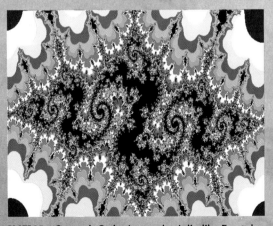

PLATE 25   Seventh Order Legendre Julia-like Fractal.

PLATE 26   Seventh Order Laguerre Julia-like Fractal.

PLATE 27   Seventh Order Hermite Julia-like Fractal.

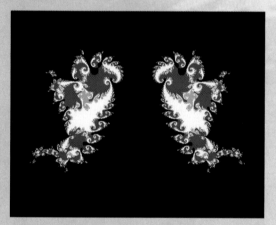

PLATE 28   Phoenix Fractal.

PLATE 29   Mandela Fractal.

PLATE 30   Pokorny Fractal with Exponent 1.

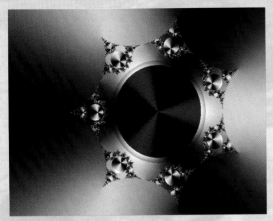

PLATE 31   Pokorny Fractal with Exponent 3.

PLATE 32   Appolonian Packing of Circles.

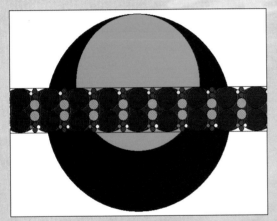

PLATE 33   Pharaoh's Breaatplae without Inversion.

PLATE 34   Pharaoh's Breastplate with Inversion.

PLATE 35   Self-Homographic Fractal.

PLATE 36   First Barnsley Fractal.

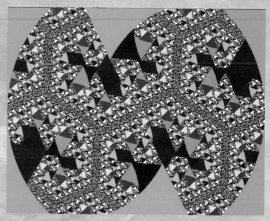

PLATE 37   Second Barnsley Fractal.

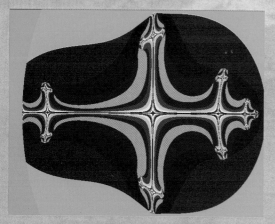

PLATE 38   Third Barnsley Fractal.

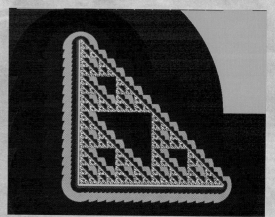

PLATE 39   Barnsley Sierpinski Triangle Fractal.

PLATE 40   Mountain Fractal.

13

What You Can Do with Mandelbrot-like and Julia-like Fractals

W e are now going to look at fractals that are generated by iterating an equation a number of times and classifying the resulting behavior. Consider, for example, the equation

$$z_{n+1} = z_n^2 + c \qquad (13.1)$$

where both z and c are complex numbers. For the first iteration of this equation, we set up a constant c and specify some initial value z_0, which we plug into the equation in place of z_n. We then solve the equation to obtain a result z_1. We then plug this value in to replace z_n, solve the equation to obtain z_2, and then repeat this process as many times as desired. We are now faced with the problem of plotting the points we get from this iteration process in a meaningful display. There are two ways of doing this. The first, originated by Mandelbrot [Mandelbrot83], is to define the display as a portion of the complex plane, with real values in the x direction and imaginary values in the y direction. For each pixel of this plane, we set the constant c to be the complex number representing the pixel, let the initial value z_0 be (0.0, 0.0), and then perform the iteration process. Generally speaking, there are two possible outcomes of the iteration process. First, the result may settle down to some constant value. Mandelbrot decided to color all pixels where the iteration had this outcome with a background color. The second possibility is that the iteration result may continue increasing, so that eventually it would reach infinity. It can be shown that if for an iteration the magnitude of the result reaches 2, with more iterations, the magnitude will eventually go to infinity. Thus, it is possible to select some threshold value greater than 2 and just stop the iteration process when this value is reached. Mandelbrot decided to cycle through the colors he had available, assigning a value to the pixel based on how many iterations had occurred when the threshold was reached. (Another way of describing this behavior is to say that one attractor for the Mandelbrot set is infinity. After we go though this procedure for every pixel on the display, we have a picture you will get a feel for this speed at which an iteration is approaching infinity by the color of the pixel. The result is the famous Mandelbrot set, which we will describe in detail in the next chapter. Note that the simple iterated equation given earlier is simply one of many that have the same type of behavior. We will look at many others in future chapters.

JULIA SETS

The Julia sets use the very same equations used for the Mandelbrot sets. However, Julia used a different method of displaying the results [Julia18]. The computer display screen again represents a portion of the complex plane. However, as we integrate for each pixel, instead of the initial value of z being set at (0.0, 0.0), it is set to the value represented by the pixel. (For the Mandelbrot set, we put this value into c.) For Julia sets, the variable c remains constant for the entire graphic, its real value corresponding to the setting of the parameter P in the program, and its imaginary value corresponding to the setting of the parameter Q. These parameters are shown in boxes at the right side of the screen so that you can enter new values there if you're creating a new Julia fractal or record them for future use if you've found a Julia fractal you especially like. We also use a different coloring technique, wherein the equation values that blow up (go toward infinity in the limit) are set to a selected background color and the remaining pixels are colored according to the value that z settles down to by the time all iterations are completed. For every Mandelbrot-like set that is included in the Fractal program and is described in the following chapters, there is at least one accompanying Julia set, which may be displayed by selecting the fractal type from the *Select Fractal Type* menu and then clicking on one of the Julia types in the submenu. We've tried to set the Julia parameters to produce Julia-like sets that you will find beautiful and interesting to look at or expand.

THE MANDELBROT SET AS A MAP OF JULIA SETS

If you want to create a Julia set from scratch, the major problem is that of defining a proper value for c. Only a few cs produce interesting Julia sets. In fact, for many values the result is a blank screen. Fortunately, the Mandelbrot set can serve as a map of useful Julia sets. Any cusp where there is a rapid change in the boundary of the Mandelbrot set represents a value of c that is likely to produce a good Julia set. The Fractal program has been set up so that when you select a cusp with the cursor and right-click, the program will create a Julia fractal using the value of c that you selected. This process will be described in greater detail in Chapter 14.

EXPANSION OF THE DISPLAY

One of the more interesting characteristics of the Mandelbrot-like and Julia-like sets is that when expanded they reveal more and more interesting and lovely detail. This detail differs for each fractal and is completely different for each additional expansion.

The Fractal program provides two methods for expanded display of this type of fractal. First, you can pick the area you want expanded by placing the cursor where you want the top left corner of the new display to be and then holding down the left mouse button while you drag the cursor down to the bottom right corner that you want for your new display. When you release the mouse button a rectangle will remain on the display showing the area that will compose the new display. The fractal will then be redrawn in expanded form. If you want a permanent record of your expansions, you can check the box labeled *Save then Expand*. Then, when you release the mouse button to mark the lower left corner of your expansion rectangle, a display will appear that allows you to save the current display with the expansion rectangle marked on it. After the saving process is complete, the expanded fractal will be drawn and displayed.

A second way to expand the display is to change the values of *XMax*, *XMin*, *YMax*, and *YMin* shown at the top of the screen. These represent the limits of the display. You can change them as you want. When you are satisfied with the new values, click on the menu item *Repeat* and the expanded fractal will be drawn. This is especially useful if you find that your expanded display has just a small portion off the screen. Just change the boundary so that the missing portion is included, then click Repeat, and the whole fractal will be displayed as you want it.

In addition to changing the bounds of a fractal by modifying the *XMax, XMin, YMax,* and *YMin* boxes, you can change the characteristics of a Julia fractal by changing the values in the Julia Dragon *P* and *Q* boxes. We have already pointed out that you can't just put any numbers into these parameters; otherwise, the result will often be just a blank screen. But if you have a Julia-like fractal that seems to be almost what you want, but lacks a little in detail, for example, you can sometimes improve it greatly by just making minor changes in these boxes. If you are going to try this, be sure to record the original values in the boxes before you try experimenting. Then, if you need to, you can get back to where you were originally.

This chapter provided an understanding of how Julia-like fractals can be created from Mandelbrot-like ones and how you can expand and change the parameters of fractals. Now we will look at some of the actual fractal equations.

REFERENCES

[Julia18] Julia, Gaston M., "Memoire sur l'iteration des functions rationales." *Journal de Mathematiques Pures et Appliques,* (1918).

[Mandelbrot83] Mandelbrot, Benoit B., *The Fractal Geometry of Nature.* W. H. Freeman and Company, 1983.

THE MANDELBROT AND JULIA SETS

G aston Julia, a French mathematician, began working with iterated functions about 1917. In the course of his work, he discovered the interesting behavior when iterated of the equation:

$$z_{n+1} = z_n^2 + c \qquad (14.1)$$

where both z and c are complex numbers. This is the basis of the Julia sets. Julia picked interesting values of the complex number c to remain constant through his computation of a picture. He then produced a graphical display by doing a set of iterations for each of a number of points in the complex plane. For each point, he set the initial value z_0 to the value of the point in the complex plane. Julia published a 199-page article in 1918 titled, "Memoire sur l'iteration des functions rationnelles" [Julia18]. Unfortunately, there were no computers available to perform Julia's calculations so he had to do everything by hand. As a result, Julia wasn't able to look as deeply into the behavior of iterated equations as he might have liked. Consequently, his interesting mathematical results were largely forgotten until the tools became available to look at them in depth.

Benoit Mandelbrot, a Fellow at the IBM Thomas J. Watson Research Center, began applying computers to perform iterations of the previous equation in the 1970s [Mandelbrot83]. Mandelbrot could obtain almost unlimited results with his computers, but he was faced with the problem of how to plot these results to provide some meaning to the observer. To do this, he decided to let his computer display represent a portion of the complex plane, with real values in the x direction and imaginary values in the y direction. Thus, each pixel on the computer display corresponds to a complex number, which Mandelbrot assigned to the parameter c in the previous equation. Letting the initial value of z be (0.0,0.0), he then colored the pixel to represent the result of the iteration process. One attractor for the Mandelbrot set is infinity. It can be shown that if the magnitude of the function ever exceeds 2, it will eventually be attracted to infinity. For such cases, we stop iterating after the value of the function has reached a predetermined point. We then take the number of iterations that it took to reach this point and consider it a measure of how fast the function is approaching infinity for this set of initial values. We then color the pixel with one of our available colors. We cycle through the colors as the speed with which the function approaches infinity changes, so that looking at the graph you can get a feel for this speed by the color of each pixel. The function never goes to infinity for some initial values but, rather, settles down to a particular value. After performing the specified number of iterations, if such a case is encountered, we color the pixel with the background color.

The Fractal program chooses default limits for the Mandelbrot set such that the real part of c varies between −2.0 and +0.9 and the imaginary part of c varies between −1.2 and +1.2. The program assumes by default that we shall run no more than 128 iterations for each pixel. If at some point in this process, the value of the equation becomes larger than 120, we can assume that it is on its way to infinity. In this case, we assign a color value to the pixel that depends on how fast it is approaching infinity. We cycle through 105 assigned colors as the speed with which the function is approaching infinity increases. The smaller the number of iterations required to reach 120, the faster is the speed at which the function approaches infinity.

By default, the Mandelbrot set is displayed when you first begin to run the Fractal program. At other times, you can call it up by selecting the fractal type *Mandelbrot* from the *Select Fractal Type* menu. In addition to changing the colors, which we'll describe in the next chapter, you can modify the Mandelbrot set in a couple of ways. First, you can change the maximum number of iterations if you want more or less detail. Simply place your cursor on the box at the right of the display labeled *Iterations* and type the maximum number of iterations that you want. Second, there is a box labeled *Mandelbrot Exponent*. By default, this box contains the exponent 2, which causes the program to work with the equation used by Julia and Mandelbrot. However, you can change this exponent to whatever integer you like. Each exponent results in a new equation with a different set of Mandelbrot and Julia displays. Plate 5 shows the Mandelbrot set as generated by the Fractal program.

PLATE 5   The Mandelbrot set.

Unfortunately, the extreme simplicity of this iterated equation tends to mask just what is happening during the iteration process. Let's take a closer look at it. We start each set of iterations with a value of (0.0, 0.0) for z_0, so the result of the first iteration is

$$z_1 = c \tag{14.2}$$

Plugging this into the second iteration, we get

$$z_2 = c^2 + c \tag{14.3}$$

For the third iteration, we have

$$z_3 = (c^2 + c)^2 + c \tag{14.4}$$

And for the fourth iteration the result is

$$z_4 = ((c^2 + c)^2 + c)^2 + c \tag{14.5}$$

For values of c greater than 1, the result of numerous iterations is that the result goes to infinity. For smaller values of c, the function settles down to some steady value. The graphing of the Mandelbrot set, which is described later, is shown in Plate 5. The boundary between the black background and the colored portions of the display marks the point at which the iteration process changes from one type of behavior to the other. You can display this fractal in your Fractal program and trace around the boundary with your cursor to see just where the transitions take place. The boxes at the right of the display that are marked X and Y show the values of the real and imaginary parts of c respectively for the current cursor position.

As we search around these boundaries when z_0 or c are complex numbers, the behavior of the equation during iteration becomes harder to figure out. For many years, no tools were available for performing the large number of iterations needed to investigate the equation's behavior in an efficient fashion. Mathematicians spent large amounts of time doing the manual calculations with limited results. Therefore, mathematicians just assumed that the equation would eventually reach some limiting values in a regular fashion. When computers made it possible to perform many iterations simply and rapidly, it was discovered that the behavior of the expression was much more complicated and that the result of performing many iterations of the expression for various values yielded fractal curves of extreme complexity, detail, and beauty.

EXPANDING THE MANDELBROT SET

We have already shown that you can provide almost unlimited expansion of the Mandelbrot set in two ways. The first method is to insert new values into the boxes labeled *XMax, XMin, YMax,* and *YMin* after displaying a fractal. These correspond to the maximum and minimum values of the real and imaginary parts of the parameter *c* respectively. You must then run the program for the same fractal type. (If you choose a different fractal type, it will show default values.) You will find this method of expansion very valuable in a couple of cases. First, if you have at some point displayed a fractal that you like and have recorded the values for these parameters, you can re-create it at any time by inserting the recorded values into the proper boxes. Also, if one of your friends has found an interesting fractal and has recorded the parameters, it's very simple for you to duplicate it. Second, if you are expanding a fractal and discover that you've cut off a portion that you really wanted to see or that you have mispositioned the fractal, you can modify the parameter in the appropriate box and run the fractal again to get the display you want.

As pointed out in the previous chapter, another way you can expand a fractal is to position your cursor where you want the top right corner of the expanded fractal to be and then hold down the left mouse button while dragging down to where you want the bottom right corner of the expanded fractal to be. As you're doing this, a dashed rectangle will show you the limits of your expanded fractal. When you release the mouse button, the expanded fractal will be drawn on the screen automatically. You can then expand any section you want of the new fractal and continue repeating this process until your computer runs out of accuracy to store the parameter. When you expand a fractal by this method, its limits will be displayed in the boxes described earlier when the expanded version of the fractal is displayed. Be sure to copy them down if you want to reproduce the fractal later. Plate 6 shows a highly expanded version of the Mandelbrot set, which demonstrates clearly the self-similarity of this fractal. Note the close similarity of the enlarged black figure in the middle of the picture to the shape of the original-sized Mandelbrot set. Plate 7 shows another enlargement of the Mandelbrot set, also demonstrating self-similarity and colored with the Gradient coloring set, which we will describe later.

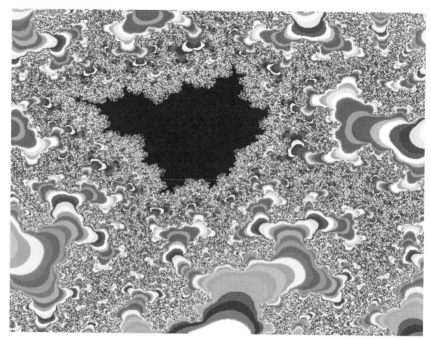

PLATE 6 Expanded Mandelbrot set showing self-similarity.

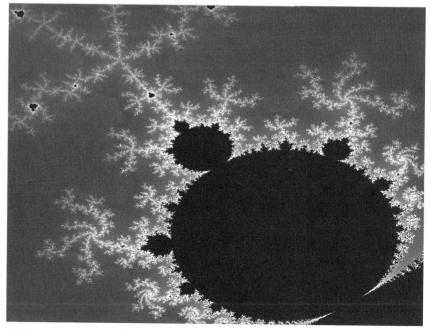

PLATE 7 Expanded Mandelbrot set with gradient coloring.

JULIA SETS

The Julia sets use the same equations used for the Mandelbrot sets, however, Julia used a different method for displaying the results. The computer display screen again represents a portion of the complex plane. As we integrate for each pixel, instead of the initial value of z being set at (0.0, 0.0), it is set to the value represented by the pixel. (For the Mandelbrot set, we would have put this value into c.) For Julia sets, the variable c remains constant for the entire graphic, its real value corresponding to the setting of the parameter P in the program and its imaginary value corresponding to the setting of the parameter Q. These parameters are shown in boxes at the top of the screen so that you can enter new values there if you're creating a new Julia fractal or record them for future use if you've found a Julia fractal you especially like. We also use a different coloring technique, wherein the equation values that blow up (go toward infinity in the limit) are set to a selected background color and the remaining pixels are colored according to the value that z settles down to by the time all iterations are completed. Plate 8 shows the first available Julia set. You may view this by choosing the Mandelbrot item from the *Select Fractal Type* menu and then choosing *Julia 1*. By selecting *Julia 2* you can view the Julia set shown in Plate 9. Finally, by selecting *Hypnoteyes,* you can view the expanded fractal that seems like a pair of staring eyes,

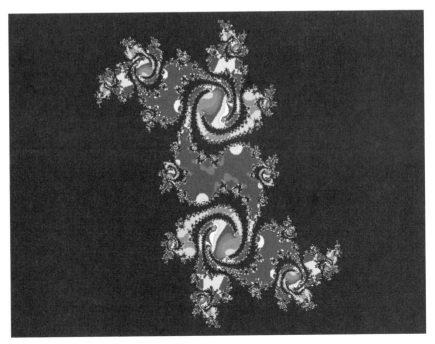

PLATE 8   Julia set 1.

PLATE 9 Julia set 2.

PLATE 10 Julia set—Hypnoteyes.

as shown in Plate 10. Note that any of these Julia fractals may be expanded in the same ways as the Mandelbrot set can be expanded. If you choose to vary the *XMax, XMin, YMax,* and *YMin* parameters to achieve expansion or change in placement, remember that you must then run the same fractal again to see the modified picture. Note also that the parameters *P* and *Q* at the top right of the display are characteristic of the particular fractal you are viewing; if you change them, you'll get something different.

THE MANDELBROT SET AS A MAP OF JULIA SETS

The primary problem in defining a Julia set is finding a suitable value for *c*. Actually, most the values that could be chosen for *c* yield only a background-colored screen (because all the equation values blow up). So how do we pick out the proper values for *c* (*P* and *Q*) so that we will get an interesting Julia set? It turns out that if you look at the Mandelbrot set, it forms a kind of a map of good Julia set *c* values. Going to the boundaries of the Mandelbrot set figure and especially choosing a point on the boundary that is a cusp (a place where a rapid change of direction takes place) usually gives a value for *c* that produces an interesting Julia set. The Fractal program allows you to do this, not only for the Julia set, but also for Julia-like sets associated with many other Mandelbrot-like fractals. To do this for Julia sets, you simply select the Mandelbrot fractal. Then, locate your cursor at the point from which you think a good Julia set can be created, and then click the right mouse button. This will create a new Julia set having the *P* and *Q* values corresponding to the location of your cursor when you right clicked. You can expand this new Julia set in the same ways that you did with others. Note that if you want to change the parameter values to alter the Julia set's position, after changing the values, you need to select a color from the *Select Color Combination* menu so the new picture can be drawn. This is because when the program sees the right-click action that produces a Julia set from the basic Mandelbrot set, it internally modifies the parameter that defines the fractal so that it is not the same as any defined in the *Select Fractal Type* menu.

NUMBER OF ITERATIONS

For some sets of parameters, the situation is a little "iffy." A situation may occur where you can get a perfectly good Julia fractal if you don't run too many iterations, but if you do run too many, the value of the iterated equation may "drift off," and finally "blow up," resulting in a screen that shows only the background color. This may be because the computer doesn't have enough precision to keep the equation values accurate for the full range of iterations. As you begin to reduce the number of iterations, you will start losing some of the fractal detail, but it still may have enough detail that you feel is satisfactory. If you encounter one of these situations, you'll have to go through a trial-and-error process. You need to keep reducing the number of iterations until you find the right value for the best results from the fractal you are working on. You do this by using the box at the middle right of the screen labeled Iterations. By default, this contains the number 128. You can enter any number you want in this box, then run the same fractal again and it will now allow the specified number of iterations. The default number of 128 is a good compromise for most fractals. If the screen is empty, reduce the number of iterations. If you want more detail, for example if the display has large blobs of the same color and appears lack detail, you can increase the number of iterations. As you increase, if the fractal begins to disappear or disappears completely, reduce the number of iterations again. A good number to begin with is 64 iterations. Then, if the display is sparse, with a large number of isolated points, you can decrease the number of iterations.

SPECIFYING JULIA SET PARAMETERS

Rather than using the Mandelbrot set to select good values of P and Q for a Julia set, you can create one of the existing Julia sets and then insert new values for P and Q, presuming that you know a pair of values that may produce a good Julia set. If you know the parameters that will create a beautiful or unusual Julia set, you can use this method to produce the fractal display. Table 14.1 shows the parameters for a number of typical Julia sets. You can create all of these using the Fractals program by displaying *Julia 1* and then inserting the specified P and Q values and choosing a color from the *Select Color Combination* menu or by selecting *Julia 1* again.

Table 14.1 Julia Set Parameters

P	Q	ITERATIONS
0.238498	0.519198	28
−0.743036	0.113467	28
−.192175	0.656734	64
0.108294	−0.670487	32
−0.392488	−0.587966	64
−0.392488	−0.587966	256

→

0.138341	0.649857	32
0.278560	−0.003483	24
−1.258842	0.065330	48
−1.028482	−0.264756	48
0.268545	−0.003483	64
0.318623	0.044699	256
0.318623	0.429799	48

HYPNOTEYES

Just by looking at the first two Julia fractals, you would never guess that hidden within their intricate structure is the strange looking fractal shown in Plate 10, which almost seems to be a set of eyes staring hypnotically at you. This fractal, called *Hypnoteyes*, was discovered by Pieter Branderhorst and can be generated by selecting the *Hypnoteyes* submenu under the Mandelbrot type in the *Select Fractal Type* menu. An alternate way to create this fractal is to run any Julia type fractal and then modify the values of six parameter boxes. The values needed are *XMax* = 0.17487, *XMin* = −0.162458, *YMax* = 0.984935, *YMin* = 0.734422, *P* = 0.258919, and *Q* = 0.0. You will also have to choose the Mandelbrot item from the *Select Color Combination* menu. Then click on *Repeat,* and *Hypnoteyes* will be generated.

BINARY DECOMPOSITION

We have seen that the Julia set uses a different way of assigning colors than the Mandelbrot set does. In Chapter 15, we describe available color combinations and how to use them. There is, however, a completely different way of coloring Julia sets, using only two colors. You'll remember that, the test for the Julia function blowing up is that the magnitude of the complex number obtained from an iteration of the equation achieves a value greater than does *a specified maximum size.* Suppose we consider the real and imaginary parts of the complex number when that magnitude is achieved. They can be considered to represent a vector in the complex plane that has a direction from the origin and a magnitude. We determine what the direction angle is, and then color the corresponding point on the Julia picture black if that angle is between 0 and 180 degrees, and white if the angle is between 180 and 360 degrees. (All points that don't blow up have an angle too, namely that of the root to which they settle down, but that information isn't interesting, so we just color it black.) We can use colors in this way by displaying a Julia fractal and then selecting *Binary Decomposition* from the *Select Color Combination* menu. Figure 14.1 shows the Julia 1 fractal displayed with this technique, Figure 14.2 shows a Julia fractal that has $P = 0.0$ and $Q = 0.0$ for its parameters as displayed with the binary decomposition technique. Note that displaying this fractal with one of the other Julia coloring methods just produces a very uninteresting circle. With the binary decomposition coloring method, considerable hidden detail is uncovered.

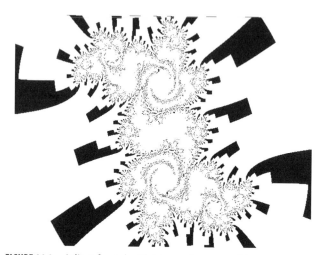

FIGURE 14.1   Julia 1 fractal with binary decomposition.

FIGURE 14.2   Julia fractal with P and $Q = 0.0$ using binary decomposition.

REFERENCES

[Julia18] Julia, Gaston M., "Memoire sur l'iteration des functions rationnelles," *Journal de Mathematiques Pures et Appliques* (1918).

[Mandelbrot83] Mandelbrot, Benoit B., *The Fractal Geometry of Nature,* W. H. Freeman and Company, 1983.

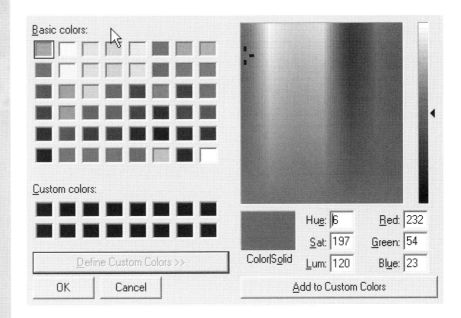

WORKING WITH COLORS

T he Fractal program includes many options for working with colors. You can achieve almost unlimited artistic effects with some of the more complex fractals once you become familiar with the various coloring modes.

COLORING L-SYSTEMS FRACTALS

Most of the fractals generated with the L-Systems approach are by default shown in the form of black lines on a white background. With just two colors involved, there isn't much opportunity for color manipulation. You can, however, choose new foreground and background colors with which to display each fractal. Simply click on the *Select Color Combination* menu, then click *Color Background,* and then select your background color. The fractal will be redrawn with the color background you select. If you don't like any of the preselected colors, you can click on the sub-menu item *Select Background Color* and a display panel will appear that allows you to choose any of a number of colors or generate your own color with precisely the red, green, and blue components that you want. Next, you can click on *Select Color Combination* again and click on *Image Color,* and choose the color you want for the foreground. The fractal will again be redrawn. The background color will be the same as you previously selected and the foreground (image) color will be that just chosen. These will remain the default colors for this kind of fractal until you choose to select others or until the program is shut down. Therefore, if you choose another L-Systems fractal, it will be drawn in the colors you selected, and you will have to reselect the colors if you want different ones. Be careful not to choose the same color for foreground and background; if you do, the fractal will be invisible.

Two fractals use combinations of previously defined fractals. The first of these is the combination of the Gosper curve and the Peano-Gosper curve. The second is the twin dragon, which is a combination of two Harter-Heighway dragon curves. Each of these uses two different colors. If you want to use something other than the default color combinations, you select an image color as described earlier. The combination fractal will be drawn with one part of the fractal drawn using a default color and the second part using the image color you just selected. Now, if you want to select a second color for one of these fractals, you can go through the process again, selecting another image color. Now the fractal will be drawn with the first image color you selected (used in place of the default color used for the first image) and the second part drawn with the second image color (the one you just selected). In planning the two colors you are going to use for the combination fractals, you need to give a little forethought to your selections. When you select the first color, it will be drawn on a part of the fractal, but when you select the second color, it will be drawn on the part of the fractal that was just drawn in the first color, and the remainder of the fractal will be drawn in the first color. The program doesn't tell you which colors are to be painted on which sections of the combination fractals; you'll need to discover this by trial and error.

MANDELBROT COLORS

For the traditional Mandelbrot set, we define our computer display to represent a section of the complex plane, with real numbers along the *x*-axis and imaginary numbers along the *y*-axis. For each pixel, we then set *z* of the Mandelbrot equation to an initial value of (0.0, 0.0) and *c* to the value represented by the pixel. We then iterate the equation until the value of *z* exceeds a threshold (indicating to us that *z* is on its way toward infinity) or until a predetermined number of iterations has occurred. The latter indicates that *z* is settling down to some limit; we color such pixels with a background color. By default, the background color is black, but you can change it by first running the Mandelbrot set fractal and then choosing the Select Color Combination menu, clicking on Color Background, and then selecting the background color you desire. When you run the Mandelbrot fractal again, the selected background color will be used. For pixels where the threshold value is reached, we take the number of iterations that are required to reach the threshold as a measure of how fast the equation is headed toward infinity. A very small number of iterations means it is going to infinity very fast indeed, whereas if many iterations are required, it is a lot slower. The Fractals program defines 106 different shades of color. To find the proper one, we take the number of iterations modulo 105 and add 1. (We don't want to cycle through the first member of the color array because this is the default background color of black.) The resulting number is the number of the member of the color array that is assigned to that pixel. This same coloring scheme is the default one used for many other fractals generated by this program that give Mandelbrot-like displays.

Many of the early fractal pictures, particularly those involving Mandelbrot sets, were created using early color monitors that were limited to 16 colors. If you'd like to use this color scheme in your fractals, it's very simple. After drawing the fractal, just enter the *Select Color Combination* menu and select *Mandelbrot 16.*

JULIA COLORS

You've already seen that the Julia set uses the same iterated equation as the Mandelbrot set does, except that we use a constant value for *c* and set *z* to the value represented by the pixel. A different coloring scheme is also used. All pixels where the iterated function exceeds the threshold, meaning that the expression is on the way to infinity, are colored with the background color. For pixels where the function is approaching a steady state value, we take the equation value modulo 15 and add 1, giving us a number from 1 to 15. This number is used to select a color from an array of 15 colors, and the pixel is colored with that color. The result is usually a beautifully colored Julia display.

Suppose we use the Julia coloring scheme to color the Mandelbrot set. The mathematics of the Mandelbrot set computations remains the same, but the method of coloring changes. The result is usually a very uninteresting set of colors. You can try it yourself and see the results. Again, suppose we use the Mandelbrot coloring scheme on a Julia set. Again, the mathematics remains that of the Julia set, but the coloring is completely different. A much more interesting picture results, but unfortunately the shape and beauty of the Julia set are somewhat obscured. You might like the effect better than the original Julia set, though.

DRAGON COLORS

Although the iterated equation is different, the self-squared dragon curve is basically a Julia set. It uses the same mathematical technique and the same coloring method. However, for the dragon set, we've assigned a palette of 16 colors that includes mostly reds, yellows, and oranges, to give the effect of a fire-breathing dragon. This color palette is automatically selected when you choose the *Dragon* fractal type. Once you've made an initial run of the dragon curve, you can select another color combination and see the different colorings available. You can also use the *Dragon* color combination with other fractals, although you might have difficulty in finding a fractal that shows them as dramatically as the dragon curve does.

PHOENIX AND PHOENIX 2 COLORS

A special technique is used for coloring the Phoenix curve, which will be described in Chapter 20. As with the Mandelbrot set, a background color is chosen for coloring all pixels where the iterated equation does not exceed a specified limit. If this limit is exceeded, the pixel is colored with one of three colors (blue, green, or yellow) depending on how many iterations were required to exceed the specified limit. You can view the Phoenix curve using this coloring by selecting *Phoenix* from the *Select Fractal Type* Menu, and then selecting *Phoenix* from the submenu. You can also use this set of colors with other fractals by selecting *Phoenix* from the *Select Color Combination* menu, although there may be some loss of detail. When you select the *Phoenix 2* fractal, a second set of colors is used. Instead of blue, yellow, and green, the color combination consists of silver, bronze, and old gold. For the background, this color combination normally uses black, but also randomly selects points of white in the black background, to simulate the effect of a night sky.

BLUE AND SILVER

This is an array of 16 colors that are all shades of blue and silver. The case works in the same way as for Mandelbrot colors. For pixels where the equation does not exceed the stated limit, the zeroeth member of the array is chosen as the background color (a dark blue). For the pixels where the equation does exceed the limit, we cycle through the remaining 15 colors to find the proper one to represent each pixel, depending on the number of iterations that occurred before the equation exceeded the limit.

RANDOM COLORS

This coloring method has a pallet of 16 colors that are used in Mandelbrot fashion. Each time you select this color combination from the *Select Color Combination* menu, the program first randomly selects one of the background colors to become the zeroeth member of *color_array[6]*. This will be used for the background (where the iteration settles down to some constant value) of the Mandelbrot set or whatever fractal you are viewing. The program then randomly rearranges the remaining 15 colors of the array. When creating a Mandelbrot type fractal, the program cycles through these colors to indicate the speed at which the iteration is approaching infinity. Once you have selected this method by choosing the menu item *Select Color Combination* and then clicking on *Random Colors,* the set of colors that were randomly selected will remain in force until you choose another color combination. If you find a set that you like, make sure to save any fractals that you create with these colors because once you select *Random Colors* again a whole new set of random colors will display and you might not see that set that you liked so well again. If you don't like the random colors that are displayed, just select *Random Colors* again and keep doing this until you get a set that you like. Note that if you find a good set of random colors and then choose a fractal that automatically uses a set of default colors, the random colors are gone forever; when you reselect *Random Colors*, a whole new random selection will occur.

If you want to use random colors applied with the Julia technique, you need to choose *Random Julia* from the *Select Color Combination* menu. This selection creates a random palette of 16 colors in the same way as described for the *Random* color selection. However, the background color is applied to all pixels where the iteration is going toward infinity and the remaining colors are used to indicate the value that the iteration settles down to otherwise.

CUSTOM COLORS

The Fractal program allows you to use the same type of 16-color palette used in the *Random* color combinations described earlier, but you can set each one of the 16 colors to exactly the shade that you want it to be. To do this, choose *Set Custom Colors* from the *Select Color Combination* menu. The menu shown in Figure 15.1 will appear superimposed on the main screen. At the bottom right of the main screen will appear a box with the legend *Color 0*. You are now required to enter 16 colors before the program will return to the main Fractal program. You can click on any of the color boxes to select a desired color. Then click on *OK*. The color you selected will be stored as *Color 0* and the box at the bottom right corner of the screen will show *Color 1*. You can now choose a color for Color 1, and so on. After you've chosen the 16th color (the box will be displaying *Color 15*) then when you click on *OK*, the color menu will disappear and you will be back in the regular Fractal program, but with your new 16-color-customized palette stored away.

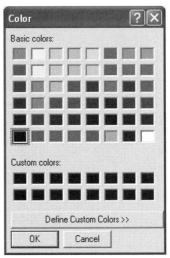

FIGURE 15.1   Menu for selecting custom colors.

If you are not satisfied with any of the colors shown in the color boxes and want to define your own exact shade, instead of clicking on a color box for the color you're working on, click on *Define Custom Colors.* The display shown in Figure 15.2 will appear. You can click on the shade you want on the right-hand part of the display and a sample will appear in the box labeled *Color Solid.* Alternatively, you can define your custom color by entering numbers in the *Hue, Saturation,* and *Luminance* boxes or the *Red, Green,* and *Blue* boxes. As you change any of these numbers, the color in the box marked *Color Solid* will change to show the exact shade you have selected. Once you have the color right, click on *Add to Custom Colors,* and your selected color will appear in the first empty box marked *Custom Colors.* You can then click on this box to choose your custom color to be added to the palette and then click *OK* to transfer it to the palette as the color number shown in the box at the lower right of the screen.

Once your custom palette is created, it will remain available until you rewrite it or until you shut down the program. You can choose to use it on an actual fractal by choosing the *Select Color Combination* menu. To use the colors in the Mandelbrot mode, click on *Use custom Colors.* To use the colors in the Julia mode, click on *Use Julia Custom Colors.*

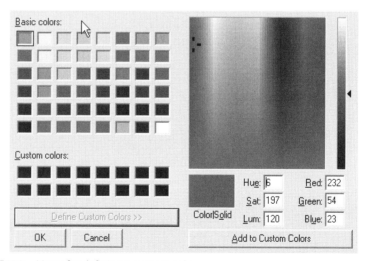

FIGURE 15.2   Menu for defining a custom color.

COMPLEX COLORS

The Fractal program includes three very complex sets of colors for use in coloring fractals. They involve manipulation of colors and hue, saturation, and luminance to produce very dramatic effects of color and shading that often appear three-dimensional. For other fractals, however, even though the three-dimensional effect is there, only a couple colors may appear. To use these effectively, you need to select the fractal you want to work with and enlarge it as you require. Then try the complex coloring scheme by choosing the *Select Color Combination* menu and then trying *Complex 1*, *Complex 2*, or *Complex 3*.

GRADIENT COLORS

The gradient combination of colors sets up 640 shades of color, which vary smoothly from one color into another. These colors are defined by six points on a curve. Table 15.1 shows the default values for the six points. Each color—red, green, and blue—is capable of a value from 0 to 255 (FF in hexadecimal). This results in a gradient that begins with dark blue, transitions through lighter and lighter blues to white, then transitions through very light yellow to darker shades of yellow and orange, then to black and finally back to the original dark blue.

Table 15.1 Default Gradient Control Points

ARRAY MEMBER	RED	GREEN	BLUE
0	0	7	100
105	32	107	203
265	237	255	255
405	255	170	0
540	0	2	0
639	0	7	100

You aren't stuck with the default values of the gradient. You have almost unlimited control of the colors. If you want to make a change, you only have to click on the box at the lower right of the screen labeled *Modify Gradient*. The display shown in Figure 15.3 will appear. This display has three panels, one each for red, green, and blue, over the whole range of array values from 0 to 639. Each panel has, as a background, the gradient color scheme for all 640 values. On top of the background, the first panel has the six control points, showing the red component of each, with red circles marking the points and a dashed white line connecting them. On top of the background, the second panel has the six control points, showing the green component of each, with green circles marking the points and a dashed white line connecting them. On top of the background, the third panel has the six control points, showing the blue component of each, with blue circles marking the points and a dashed white line connecting them. The first and last control points always remain as the 0th and 639th members of the array respectively. You can't move these laterally, but you can click on the red, green, or blue circle assigned to the point, hold the mouse button down, and move up or down to increase or decrease the component of the color you have selected. For the four in-between control points, you can change the selected color component as just described, and you can move them to the right or left to change the control point position in the array. When you do this, the control point will move right or left on all three panels at the same time, regardless of which panel you are working with.

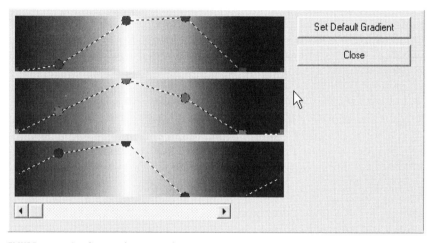

FIGURE 15.3   Gradient color controls.

Below the three panels is a scroll button that can be used to select the starting point of the gradient array. When you click on this, hold the mouse button down, and drag it between the two extremes, it chooses the point at which the array will begin. When the array gets to its end, it will recycle with the same gradient pattern you were using. New versions of the control points will be shown so that you can change them as if you had not scrolled the display. Note, however, that the new colored circles and their associated dashed lines still represent the same control points, even though they have moved toward the end of the display. Consequently, the same rules apply. Control points 0 and 5, although they now appear to be in the middle of the display cannot be moved laterally, but can be moved up or down. All other points can be moved in any direction. Finally, when you are satisfied that the gradient colors are just the way you want them, click on *Close* and the gradient display will disappear, but the new gradient array will be saved so you can work with it.

Select a fractal type, then from the *Select Color Combination* menu choose *Gradient* to use these colors with the Mandelbrot technique or choose Julia Gradient to use them with the Julia technique.

If you have modified the gradient to the extent where you just want to get back to the way it was originally, you can achieve this by clicking on *Default Gradient* in the *Select Color Combination* menu, or alternatively by clicking on *Default Gradient* while you are in the *Modify Gradient* display.

BINARY DECOMPOSITION

In Chapter 14, we introduced a technique called binary decomposition, which can be used with Julia-type fractals. This technique uses only two colors, black and white. Which is used for a particular pixel is based on the angle defined by the complex value of the iteration result. This color combination (if you'd call it that) is available by selecting the item *Binary Decomposition* from the *Select Color Combination* menu.

NEWTON COLORS

In Chapter 12, we pointed out that a special set of colors had been developed for displaying the Newton's method fractal resulting from applying Newton's method to the equation:

$$z_n^3 - 1 = 0 \qquad (15.1)$$

This combination of colors consists of various shades of the colors red, green, and blue. Each set is used for coloring an initial pixel value that converges to one of the three roots of the equation. As soon as we depart from this particular equation, the mathematical meaning represented by these sets of root-related colors is no longer applicable, but the color combination can still be used to color other fractals with some very interesting results. You can try this by running a fractal and then choosing *Newton Colors* from the *Select Color Combination* menu.

LYAPUNOV COLORS

The default color combination for the Lyapunov fractals consists of a gradient that goes through the entire rainbow in 400 steps. This set of colors will not work with any other type of fractal. You can also select the *Gradient* color combination for use with the Lyapunov fractals and then modify the gradient in any way you want.

FRACTALS WITH THE LOGISTIC EQUATION

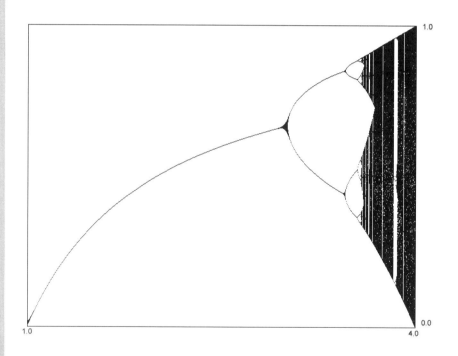

In this chapter, we are going to look at an equation that is the basis for three very different kinds of fractals. The equation is the following:

$$x_{n+1} = rx_n(1 - x_n) \tag{16.1}$$

This formula is also known as "Verhultz dynamics." It is one of the simplest known formulas for describing a chaotic dynamic system. Such a system is one in which a relationship exists that permits iteration; in other words, given an initial value, there is an equation that relates this to the next value of the variable, and this process may be repeated as many times as wanted. A whole theory attempts to determine the value of the variable as a result of the iteration process. Does it blow up to infinity? Does it converge to a stable value? Does it assume some sort of periodic behavior? Or does it seem to have totally chaotic behavior?

In 1798, Thomas Malthus made the first well-known attempt to apply mathematics to the growth and decline of populations. In his paper, "An Essay on the Principle of Population As It Affects the Future Improvement of Society," [Malthus98]. Malthus presented the proposition that population, if unchecked, grows in a geometric manner but the growth of available food supplies is arithmetic.

Consequently, unless strict birth control measures were introduced, Malthus foresaw extended calamity and widespread starvation. Fortunately for us, and unfortunately for the validity of Malthus' theory, improvements in food production techniques kept pace with population growth and the disaster never occurred. Consequently, Malthus' theory has been out of favor for a number of years. Just a few years ago, however, the Club of Rome commissioned a massive computer model to model the future of the world. Its first runs predicted that population increases would reach the limit of earthly resources and cause, by the year 2000, the kind of catastrophes that Malthus predicted. Thus, the Malthusian predictions gained a new lease on life. However, the year 2000 came and went without any sign of the great disasters that the computer model had predicted. So we cannot take these models as correct predictors of what is happening in the world, but the equations are still an interesting mathematical study.

By the early 1950s, this equation was being used by ecologists as a simplified representation of population growth. Each iteration of the equation is supposed to represent a generation of population history. The factor r is the fecundity factor, a measure of the capability of the population to reproduce. If this is less than 1 and the population is small (the x_n factor), the population will ultimately die out. Also, the $(1 - x_n)$ factor limits uncontrolled growth; as x_n approaches 1, the population again dies out. This implies that the larger the population becomes, the more forces are applied to reduce growth, such as the lack of sufficient food. Generally speaking, using this equation (particularly if the parameter r is less than one) causes the population to reach a maximum when x is equal to 0.5. If the population dies out (x decreases to zero), it, of course, never recovers and the species is extinct.

Strangely enough, everyone assumed that this equation was well behaved, and for a long time, no one discovered the chaotic behavior that could occur when r took on larger values. This is one of those things that common sense makes obvious once the facts are discovered. We have things like the seven-year locusts, which have a tremendous population explosion every seven years. Surely such examples should have made us suspect that a population value could achieve a stability with more than one stable value and shift back and forth between these values in successive iterations. But not until 1971 did Robert May, at the Institute for Advanced Study at Princeton, study this equation in detail for a wide range of values of r and at last began to understand the complicated behavior that was hidden in the simple expression.

Bifurcation Diagrams

The best way to make sense of the really complicated behavior of the simple equation is using a graph. These graphs are usually referred to as *bifurcation diagrams*. If you select the fractal type *Bifurcation Diagram* from the *Select Fractal Type* menu, you will see a graph of this fractal over a range of rs from 1.0 to 4.0. We set r to be the value represented by x for each pixel and for each *iteration;* we will start with the nominal value of 0.5 for x. The program performs 8192 iterations, each time finding a new value of x in the population equation from the previous value. If x becomes very large or very small (so that the computer can't handle the number), the iteration process is terminated. The final value of x_{n+1} after each set of iterations is plotted. For the smaller values of r, everything is well behaved, we find that x has settled to a single value. But at some point, there are two final values for x, then four, then eight, and so forth.

The default run of this subroutine uses the x-axis range of values (values of r) from 1.0 to 4.0 and the y-axis range of values from 0.0 to 1.0 (values of x_{n+1}). The resulting diagram is shown in Figure 16.1. You should note that when these bifurcations begin to occur, we no longer can apply the equation results to the real world. Population growth cannot just split into two paths, one leading to further growth and the other to extinction. And if this were the case, we would have no mathematical way of determining which path the population would actually follow.

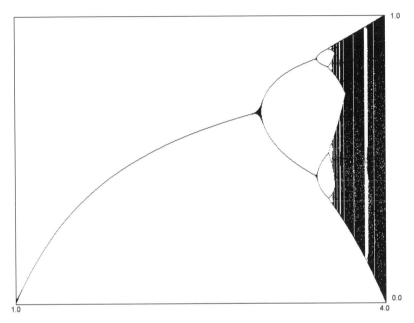

FIGURE 16.1 Bifurcation diagram.

EXPANSION OF THE DISPLAY

The same methods that the Fractal program uses to expand Mandelbrot-like and Julia-like sets also work with the bifurcation diagram. You can pick the area you want expanded by placing the cursor where you want the top left corner of the new display to be and then holding down the left mouse button while you drag the cursor down to the bottom right corner that you want for your new display. When you release the mouse button, a rectangle will remain on the display showing the area that constitutes the new display, and the program will proceed to draw the expanded fractal and display it on the screen. Another way to expand the display is to change the values of *XMax, XMin, YMax,* and *YMin* shown at the top of the screen. These represent the limits of the display. You can change them as you desire and then run *Bifurcation Diagram* again to create a display with the new limits. This is especially useful if you find that your expanded display has just a small portion off the screen. Just change the boundary so that the missing portion is included and run the fractal again. Three examples of expanded displays are shown in Figures 16.2, 16.3 and 16.4. The numbers shown in the figures do not actually appear on the displays but are given in the boxes labeled *XMax, XMin, YMax,* and *YMin* at the top of the display. You can type new values into these boxes before starting the new run (for example, you may select the values given in Figures 16.2, 16.3, or 16.4, to duplicate one of these figures).

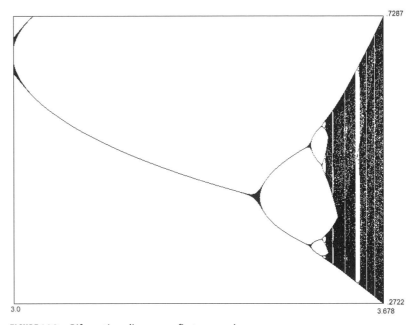

.7287

.2722

3.0

3.678

FIGURE 16.2　Bifurcation diagram—first expansion.

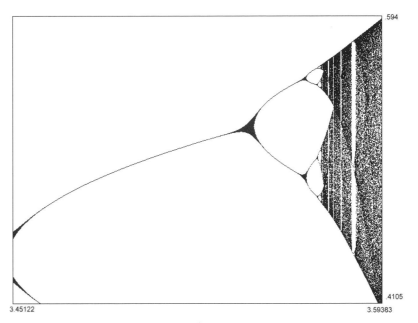

.594

.4105

3.45122

3.59383

FIGURE 16.3　Bifurcation diagram—second expansion.

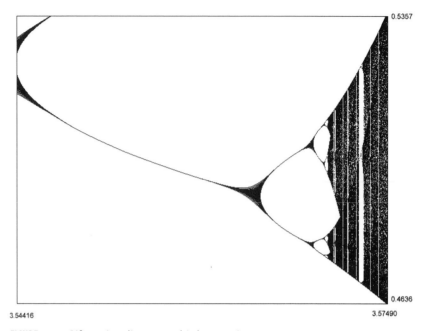

FIGURE 16.4 Bifurcation diagram—third expansion.

"Period Three Implies Chaos"

Robert May's friend James Yorke did a rigorous mathematical analysis of the behavior of the population equation and in December 1975, together with Tien-Yien Li, published an article called, "Period Three Implies Chaos." What Yorke and Li were able to show is that if a function similar to the population equation has a period of three, then it has periods of every other number, n. Thus, it is rigorously established that there is an infinitely rich spectrum of results for this type of equation. For the logistic equation, it can be shown that the behavior of the equation is chaotic whenever the parameter r exceeds 3.56994571869.

The Feigenbaum Number

At about the same time, Mitchell Feigenbaum was also investigating the population equation. Feigenbaum was trying to determine the values of the r at which the maximum is reached for each set of bifurcations. If we start with the maximum value of x and perform 2^n iterations, where n is the number of bifurcations, we should cycle through all the bifurcated values of x and be back to the maximum again. Thus, we have the general expression:

$$x_{max} = (r_n f)^{2m^n}(x_{max}) \qquad (16.2)$$

which for the population equation is as follows:

$$x_{max} = [r_n x_{max}(1 - x_{max})]^{2m^n} \qquad (16.3)$$

This equation can be solved easily for x_0 and with more difficulty for x_1, but it very quickly gets so complicated and has so many roots that a solution becomes nearly impossible.

Feigenbaum was doing this tediously on a programmable calculator. In looking for a way to reduce the number of calculations, he discovered a remarkable universal relationship between adjacent roots. This is expressed as the Feigenbaum number:

$$(r_n - r_{n-1})/r_{n+1} - r_n) = 4.6692016091029... \qquad (16.4)$$

The Feigenbaum number is an irrational number whose value is that obtained when n is equal to infinity, so that the first few values are not very precise. Feigenbaum later discovered that this universal ratio applies to every kind of iterated function that is characterized by having a single differentiable maximum. This includes many different kinds of algebraic equations as well as trigonometric equations that use only a single hump of the curve.

SELF-SQUARED DRAGONS

We've seen that simple plotting of the equation given at the beginning of this chapter yields a fractal curve that has some very unexpected characteristics. Now suppose that we take another approach and plot the results of iterating this equation using the same methodology that was used in Chapter 14 to create Julia sets. To do this, we replace r with the complex number c and replace x with the complex number z. We let our computer display represent a section of the complex plane, and for each pixel, we iterate using the complex value represented by the pixel as the initial value for z. We can get some very interesting fractal curves in this way. One of the prettiest and most dragonlike curves is obtained by allowing c to take on the value (1.6493, 0.961). Coloring pixels for which the iteration goes to infinity black and those that settle to some value with dragonlike shades of red, orange, and yellow, depending on the value the iteration settles on, we get the lovely fractal curve shown in Plate 11. Mandelbrot first discovered this. He called it the "self-squared" dragon. To complicate matters, Mandelbrot calls all of the curves that are produced from variations of the logistic equation "dragons" even though some of them do not look anything like dragons, thus making the whole classification a little confusing.

PLATE 11 Self-squared dragon.

To reiterate, the figures that Mandelbrot calls "self-squared dragons" result from iterations of the expression

$$z_{n+1} = cz_n(1-z_n) \tag{16.5}$$

where both z and c are complex numbers, the number c being represented in our program by $c = p + iq$. You will note that if both c and z are real, the equation is the same as that for the population growth curve. Observe that when you have an equation like this, where c is a multiplier instead of being added to the equation, there is no problem while attempting to create Julia-like sets because for almost every pixel z is assigned some value. But when we try to use the same equation to generate a Mandelbrot-like set, we get absolutely nothing because every time the iteration process takes place using

$$z_0 = (0.0, 0.0) \tag{16.6}$$

we find that z remains at this initial value no matter how many iterations we perform. By assigning a value slightly above zero to z for this situation, we can get a Mandelbrot-like version of the curve, but the resulting curve does not act as a map of possible dragon curves. Therefore, we have not included this curve in the program.

LYAPUNOV FRACTALS

Suppose that instead of using a fixed value of r in the logistic equation, we have several values available for this parameter, and with each iteration, we choose one of them according to a fixed pattern. We call this forcing the fractal. We also want to determine a color for coloring each pixel based on some characteristic of the behavior of the equation after a number of iterations. Lyapunov, a Russian mathematician at the beginning of the century, developed an expression that could be obtained from the logistic equation that is called the Lyapunov exponent. The expression is

$$lyap = \sum_{m=1}^{n} ((\log |r - 2rx_m|) / \log 2) / n \qquad (16.7)$$

where n is the maximum number of iterations. This expression has the characteristic of being negative when the system is stable and positive when the system is in the process of becoming chaotic. We have created a rainbow gradient for coloring the Lyapunov fractals—whenever the exponent is positive (a prediction of chaos), we color the pixel with a background color; otherwise, we select one of the gradient of colors based on the size of the exponent. This coloring technique is used by default when the Lyapunov fractal type is selected. If you want to experiment with other color combinations, after first running the Lyapunov fractal, you can select *Gradient* from the *Select Color Combination* menu and then click on *Repeat* to produce a Lyapunov fractal colored with the Gradient colors. You are then free to click on the *Modify Gradient* box and change the Gradient colors as you desire. The other color schemes in the *Select Color Combination* menu don't work with the Lyapunov fractal and are therefore disabled when that fractal is selected. The first thorough investigation of Lyapunov fractals was by Mario Markus of the Max Planck Institute for Nutrition in the late 1980s. An article called, "Leaping into Lyapunov Space," by A. K. Dewdney in the September 1991 *Scientific American* [Dewdney91] showed a number of Lyapunov fractals and assigned names to them. We have used these names in the Fractal program. You can display any of these fractals by selecting *Lyapunov* from the *Select Fractal Type* menu and then choosing the Lyapunov fractal you want to display. You can expand any of these using the same techniques described for expanding the Mandelbrot and Julia sets. When you have created one of these fractals, the string used to create the forcing pattern is shown in a box at the lower right of the display labeled *Lyapunov Sequence*. When selecting a Lyapunov fractal, you can also enter a sequence in this box and then choose the Lyapunov type *Select Sequence*, in which case your own forcing pattern will be used to create a new Lyapunov fractal. Table 16.1 shows the sequences that are used for the Lyapunov fractals that are available in the Fractal program menu. Markus set his computer to perform 600 iterations of each pixel point to let the exponent value settle down and then 4000 more to establish the value of the exponent for the pixel he wanted to color. This requires quite a bit of time to create each display. The Fractal program is set up to run one-eighth of the maximum number of iterations to get the exponent to settle down before using the rest of the iterations to determine the value of the exponent. Using the default value of 128 for maximum iterations creates reasonably good Lyapunov displays. They are a bit lacking in detail, however, so you might use the 128 value when you're looking at the fractals. If you find one you really want to print out and save, you then change the number in the *Maximum iterations* box to a much higher number and run the program again to create your final display. Plate 12 shows the Lyapunov fractal that Dewdney called the Swallow. Plate 13 shows the Lyapunov fractal that Dewdney called *Zircon Zity*.

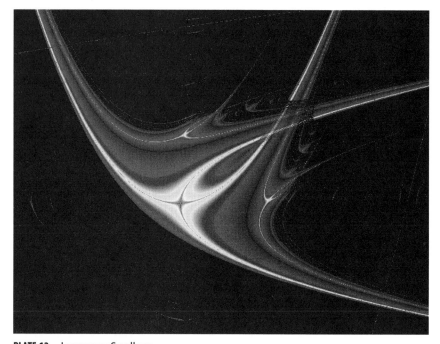

PLATE 12   Lyapunov Swallow.

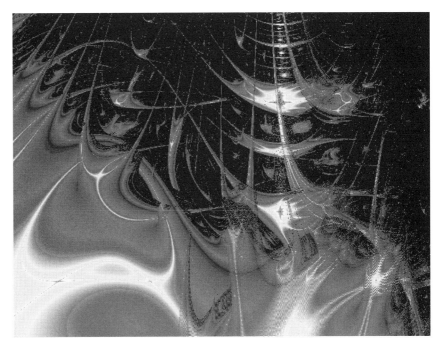

PLATE 13   Lyapunov Zircon Zity.

An interesting question arises about what might happen if instead of using a repeated pattern to force the Lyapunov fractal, one were to randomly select which forcing value to use. You might think that the forcing function patterns actually depend on the relative frequency of one forcing function with respect to the other, in which case you would get one of the existing fractal patterns. But we have already seen that the repeated pattern *ab* used for the Lyapunov Space fractal gives a far different result from the Zircon Zity pattern, which consists of repeating six *b*'s followed by six *a*'s. So this might lead you to decide that each generation of random forcing functions would give you a new and unique fractal. But you'd be wrong again. It appears that using two forcing functions in a totally random selection pattern has its own attractor that produces a unique fractal that is the same no matter what random order is used. So far, almost no mathematical analysis of this situation has taken place.

Table 16.1 Sequences for Lyapunov Fractals	
FRACTAL NAME	**SEQUENCE**
Jellyfish	bbaba
Swallow	ba
Lyapunov Space	ab →

Zircon Zity	bbbbbbaaaaaa
Hess 3	bbaba
Hess 5	aaaaaaaaaaaaaaaaaaaaaab
Hess 6	aaaaaaaaaaaab
Hess 7	bbbbbaaaaa
Markus 7a	bbababa
Markus 7b	bbababa

REFERENCES

[Dewdney91] Dewdney, A. K., "Leaping into Lyapunov Space," *Scientific American* (September 1991): pp. 178–180.

[Li75] Li, Tien-Yien, and Yorke, James A., "Period Three Implies Chaos," *Transactions of the American Mathematical Society* (December 1975): pp. 985–992.

[Malthus98] Thomas Robert Malthus, *First Essay on Population,* 1798. Macmillian, London, Publication year 1926.

17

FRACTALS USING TRANSCENDENTAL FUNCTIONS

Most of us are somewhat familiar with transcendental functions. We know that if you select an angle of a right triangle, the sine is the ratio of the opposite side to the hypotenuse and the cosine is the ratio of the adjacent side to the hypotenuse. We know how to use tables of these function values to solve various types of problems. In fact, if you were to look inside the Fractal program, you would find that it makes extensive use of sines and cosines in creating the fractals that use the L-Systems methodology. But can these functions also be used to create fractals such as the Mandelbrot and Julia sets that we have seen in previous chapters? One way to investigate this is to take advantage of the fact that each transcendental function can be represented by a Taylor series. The appropriate series are as follows:

$$\cos x = 1 - x^2/2! + x^4/4! - x^6/6! + \dots \tag{17.1}$$

$$\sin x = x - x^3/3! + x_5/5! - x^7/7! + \dots \tag{17.2}$$

$$e^x = 1 + x + x^2/2! + x^3/3! + x^4/4! + \dots \tag{17.3}$$

$$\sinh x = x + x^3/3! + x^5/5! + x^7/7! + \dots \tag{17.4}$$

$$\cosh x = 1 + x^2/2! + x^4/4! + x^6/6! + \dots \tag{17.5}$$

These equations are very similar to those we have worked with. Actually, if we truncate some of them to a couple of terms, we can use the resulting expressions to produce fractals that are almost exactly like the Mandelbrot set. For the series to give an exact value for its associated transcendental function, however, we need to extend it to an infinite number of terms. Just a few terms can produce results that are very close to the exact values and are good enough for most practical purposes. You should also note that the numbers used for x are in radians. So in this situation we need to get over any bias we might have for expressing angles in degrees. A full circle of 360 degrees corresponds to 2π or 6.283058 radians. Thus, we must train ourselves to write 1.5707645 radians rather than 90 degrees.

Another problem may arise in using transcendental functions to create fractals. We are in the habit of using complex variables in our fractal computations. It's a little hard to visualize exactly what the sine or cosine of a complex number looks like. However, some trigonometric identities can give us a better picture of what these functions look like when used with complex numbers. If $z = x + iy$ the identities are as follows:

$$\cos(x+iy) = \cos(x)\,\cosh(y) - i\,\sin(x)\,\sinh(y) \tag{17.6}$$

$$\sin(x+iy) = \sin(x)\,\cosh(y) + i\,\cos(x)\,\sinh(y) \tag{17.7}$$

$$\cosh(x+iy) = \cosh(x)\cos(y) + i\sinh(x)\sin(y) \tag{17.8}$$

$$\sinh(x+iy) = \sinh(x)\cos(y) + i\cosh(x)\sin(y) \tag{17.9}$$

$$e^{ix} = \cos(x) + i\sin(x) \tag{17.10}$$

$$e^{(x+iy)} = e^x(\cos(y) + i\sin(y)) \tag{17.11}$$

If we were using a compiler that didn't understand how to obtain the transcendental functions of complex numbers, we would have to include these expressions in our mathematical formulation of fractal-iterated equations. Fortunately, the Borland C++ Builder compiler that was used to generate the Fractal program has built-in the capability to handle complex numbers, which makes generating fractal transcendental equations easy.

COSINE FRACTAL

The iterated equation for the cosine fractal is as follows:

$$z_{n+1} = \cos(z_n) + c \tag{17.12}$$

You can view the Mandelbrot-like set produced by this equation by selecting *Cosine* from the *Select Fractal Type* menu, and then clicking *Cosine* in the submenu under that. There is also an expanded version of the cosine fractal available by clicking on *Select Fractal Type,* then on *Cosine,* and then on *Cosine Expanded.* This fractal also gives a very beautiful rendition when you color it by clicking *Select Color Combination* and then *Complex 3.* Plate 14 shows the expanded cosine fractal. To view the Julia-type cosine fractal display, select *Cosine* from the *Select Fractal Type* menu, and then click *Cosine Julia* in the submenu under that. Note that like the Mandelbrot set, the cosine fractal may be expanded by entering new parameters in the boxes at the top of the screen or by creating a rectangle by holding down the mouse button and dragging on the screen display. You can also generate new Julia-type cosine fractals by bringing up the original cosine fractal and then right-clicking on a likely looking cusp of the display. Plate 15 shows a Julia-like cosine fractal that uses the parameters *XMax* = 5.7508, *XMin* = –6.2649, *YMax* = 2.622, *YMin* = 2.276, *P* = –5.4, and *Q* = 1.51. The blue and silver color scheme was used.

PLATE 14 Expanded cosine fractal.

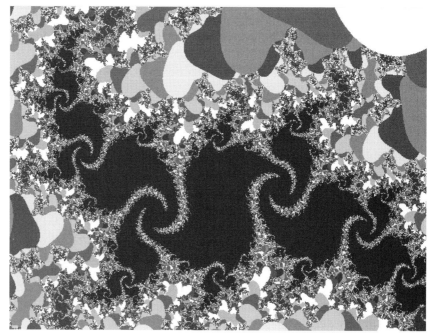

PLATE 15 Cosine Julia-like fractal.

SINE FRACTAL

The iterated equation for the sine fractal is as follows:

$$z_{n+1} = \sin(z_n) + c \qquad\qquad (17.13)$$

You can view the Mandelbrot-like set produced by this equation by selecting *Sine* from the *Select Fractal Type* menu and then clicking *Sine* in the submenu under that. An expanded version of the sine fractal that can be viewed by selecting the *Sine Fractal* and then choosing *Sine Expanded* in the submenu. Plate 16 shows the expanded sine fractal. To view the Julia-type sine fractal display, select *Sine* from the *Select Fractal Type* menu, and then click *Sine Julia* in the submenu under that. As with the cosine fractal, you can expand the fractal by putting values into the boxes at the top of the screen or by creating a rectangle on the screen by dragging the mouse. You can also select a likely set of parameters for the Julia-type sine fractal by right-clicking on the original sine fractal display. Plate 17 shows a Julia-like sine fractal that uses the parameters *XMax* = 0.71467, *XMin* = −1.0965, *YMax* = 1.4031, *YMin* = −0.5, P = 3.57125, and *Q* = −.44467. The gradient color scheme was used.

PLATE 16   Expanded sine fractal.

PLATE 17   Sine Julia-like fractal.

HYPERBOLIC COSINE FRACTAL

The iterated equation for the hyperbolic cosine fractal is as follows:

$$z_{n+1} = \cos h(z_n) + c \tag{17.14}$$

You can view the Mandelbrot-like set produced by this equation by selecting *Hyperbolic Cosine* from the *Select Fractal Type* menu and then clicking *Hyperbolic Cosine* in the submenu under that. To view the Julia-type hyperbolic cosine fractal display, select *Hyperbolic Cosine* from the *Select Fractal Type* menu, and then click *Hyperbolic Cos Julia* in the submenu under that. The same methods described for the two previous fractals can be used for expansion and for finding a likely Julia set from the parent fractal. Plate 18 shows a Julia-like hyperbolic cosine fractal that uses the parameters *XMax* = 1.456, *XMin* = –2.1, *YMax* = 0.5396, *YMin* = 0.01458, *P* = –2.181, and *Q* = 0.58333. The Random color scheme was used.

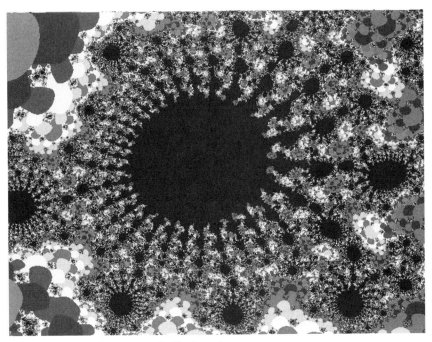

PLATE 18   Hyperbolic cosine Julia-like fractal.

HYPERBOLIC SINE FRACTAL

The iterated equation for the hyperbolic sine fractal is as follows:

$$z_{n+1} = \sinh(z_n) + c \qquad (17.15)$$

You can view the Mandelbrot-like set produced by this equation by selecting *Hyperbolic Sine* from the *Select Fractal Type* menu, and then clicking *Hyperbolic Sine* in the submenu under that. The same methods described for the previous fractals can be used for expansion and for finding a likely Julia set from the parent fractal. To view the Julia-type sine fractal display, select *Hyperbolic Sine* from the *Select Fractal Type* menu, and then click *Hyperbolic Sine Julia* in the submenu under that. Plate 19 shows a Julia-like hyperbolic sine fractal that uses the parameters *XMax* = 1.584, *XMin* = –0.1656, *YMax* = 4.547, *YMin* = 3.191, *P* = 1.1969, and *Q* = 4.6344. The Random color scheme was used.

PLATE 19   Hyperbolic sine Julia-like fractal.

Exponential Fractal

This is a good time to compare the vastly different results in the set of color plates for transcendental functions with those defining equations given in Equations 17.1 through Equation 17.5. You will note that relatively insignificant changes in signs and exponents result in fractal patterns that are quite different from each other. When we want to write an expression for the exponential fractal, things are quite different. With all the previous transcendental function iteration expressions, we have applied the function to the current variable value and then added the complex variable c. When you do this in the exponential case, the resulting fractals are very uninteresting. To get more interesting fractals for this case, we have used c as a multiplier, instead of adding it in. The resulting iterated equation for the exponential fractal is as follows:

$$z_{n+1} = c \exp(z_n) \tag{17.16}$$

You can view the Mandelbrot-like set produced by this equation by selecting *Exponential* from the *Select Fractal Type* menu, and then clicking *Exponential* in the submenu under that. The same methods described for the previous fractals can be used for expansion and for finding a likely

Julia set from the parent fractal. To view the Julia-type exponential fractal display, select *Exponential* from the *Select Fractal Type* menu, and then click *Exponential Julia* in the submenu under that. Plate 20 shows a Julia-like exponential fractal that uses the parameters *XMax* =1.4867, *XMin* = −1.6695, *YMax* = −0.924, *YMin* = −3.58, *P* = 0.33, and *Q* = −2.424. The Random color scheme was used.

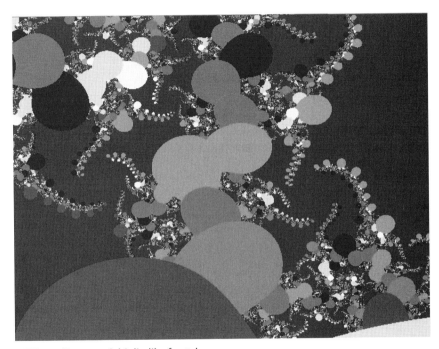

PLATE 20 Exponential Julia-like fractal.

FRACTALS USING ORTHOGONAL POLYNOMIALS

In the past few chapters, you've seen how we iterated some very sim-ple equations to produce lovely fractal pictures. If this can be done with simple equations, one might think that allowing the equations to become more complicated would result in even more beautiful fractal pictures. However, not every polynomial results in a beautiful fractal pic-ture when iterated. Actually, most polynomials that you select by chance result in uninteresting displays, many of them with a blank screen. Deter-mining the suitability of a polynomial for creating fractals is somewhat of a trial-and-error process. However, those functions defined as orthogonal polynomials have been found to be excellent candidates for generating interesting fractals. Most orthogonal polynomials have arisen from the study of the solutions of differential equations. A system of polynomials is considered to be orthogonal with respect to a weight function $w(x)$ if over the interval $a < x < b$ the following relationship holds:

$$\int_a^b w(x) f_n(x) f_m(x) dx = 0 \tag{18.1}$$

where $n \neq m$. This definition can result in many different polynomials, de-pending on what weight function is selected. One way that we can apply some standardization to orthogonal polynomials is by requiring them to fulfill the following definitions:

$$\int_a^b w(x) f_n^2(x) dx = h_n \tag{18.2}$$

$$f_n(x) = k_n x^n + k_n' x^{n+1} + \dots \tag{18.3}$$

Several interesting relationships are fulfilled by orthogonal polyno-mial systems. The first is the differential equation

$$g_2(x) f_n'' + g_1(x) f_n' + a_n f_n = 0 \tag{18.4}$$

where $g_2(x)$ and $g_1(x)$ are independent of n, and a_n is a constant depend-ing solely on n. Orthogonal polynomials also obey the recurrence rela-tionship:

$$f_{n+1} = (a_n + x b_n) f_n - c_{n-1} \tag{18.5}$$

where

$$b_n = k_{n+1} / k_n \tag{18.6}$$

$$a_n = b_n (k_{n+1}' / k_{n+1} - k_n' / k_n) \tag{18.7}$$

$$c_n = (k_{n+1} k_{n-1} h_n) / (k_n^2 h_{n-1}) \tag{18.8}$$

A good source of orthogonal polynomials is a book called *Handbook of Mathematical Functions* that was first issued by the United States National Bureau of Standards in June 1964 [Abramowitz64]. You can get a copy of this book at a reasonable price from the Superintendent of Documents at the U.S. Government Printing Office. It was the source for the equations used for all the fractals described in this chapter. The equation sets that we are going to discuss are the Bernoulli polynomials, the Chebyshev *C* polynomials, the Chebyshev *S* polynomials, the Chebyshev *T* polynomials, the Chebyshev *U* polynomials, the Legendre functions, the Laguerre polynomials, and the Hermite polynomials. The Fractals program allows you to select the second order through the seventh order of each of these polynomials and use them to create fractals.

CREATING FRACTALS WITH ORTHOGONAL POLYNOMIALS

Fractals are created with orthogonal polynomials in the usual manner, namely at each point over a selected area of the complex plane an iterated equation is evaluated and the color of the corresponding pixel is set according to the behavior of the equation. In Chapters 14 and 16, we have seen two ways for creating an iterated function that can be used to generate a fractal. We can take a polynomial and add a constant, c, or we can multiply the polynomial by c. In other words, for Mandelbrot-like sets, the iterated equation starts with z set at (0.0, 0.0) and a constant c whose value is based on the location of the pixel being processed in the complex plane and computes a new value of z equal to the orthogonal polynomial of the old z. The constant c, which is determined by the position on the complex plane, can either be added to the polynomial or multiplied by the polynomial. For Julia-like sets, we set z^0 to the value represented by the pixel and choose a fixed value for c that remains the same throughout the entire iteration process. Usually, either adding c or multiplying by it, but not both, will yield an interesting looking fractal set. When using the Julia generating technique, adding c usually results in Julia-like sets, and multiplying by c yields dragonlike sets. You have to try both ways and see which sets you like best. Either of these techniques works fine in creating Julia-like fractals. For Mandelbrot-like fractals, however, when you are multiplying the expression by c, if the orthogonal polynomial does not contain a z^0 (constant) term, you'll get a blank screen, because beginning a set of iterations with $z^0 = (0.0, 0.0)$ will result in z remaining at zero no matter how many times we can iterate. You can try the math with one of the orthogonal polynomials to verify that this is true. To avoid this problem, we add a bias (1.0 for most of the fractal equations in this chapter). This results in an expression, which is not necessarily quite a true orthogonal equation, but does give us good fractal images. For example, the Chebyshev T fourth-order polynomial, T_5 is

$$T_5 = 16z^5 - 20z^3 + 5z \tag{18.9}$$

The version that we use for the iterated equation is

$$z = c(16z^5 - 20z^3 + 5z) + 1.0 \tag{18.10}$$

Note that without the added constant of 1.0, z never changes from its initial value of (0.0, 0.0), no matter how many times you iterate.

The Fractals program allows you to select the second order through the seventh order of each of these polynomials. For each one, the first selection creates a Mandelbrot-like set. As with previous Mandelbrot-like fractals that we have discussed, you can use the mouse to select the top left corner and then drag to the bottom right corner a portion of this set. The rectangle you select will be delineated on the screen by a dashed rectangle. When you release the mouse button, this portion of the fractal will be enlarged to fill the whole screen. You can repeat this process as many times as you want. Alternately, you can insert new limit numbers in the *XMax, XMin, YMax,* and *YMin* boxes at the top of the screen, and then click on the *Result* menu to obtain a picture that fills the new limits. If you move the cursor to a cusp on a Mandelbrot-like set and then click the right mouse button, you will generate a Julia-like fractal having the P and Q coordinates of the location you selected with the cursor.

Most of the fractals in the Fractal program that are derived from orthogonal polynomials use the technique of multiplying the orthogonal polynomial by c and then adding a constant, which usually has the value 1.0.

BERNOULLI FRACTALS

The Fractals program allows you to create fractals using the second-order through seventh-order Bernoulli polynomials as iterated equations. These polynomials are as follows:

$$B_2 = z^2 - z + 1/6 \tag{18.11}$$

$$B_3 = z^3 - 3z^2/2 + z/2 \tag{18.12}$$

$$B_4 = z^4 - 2z^3 - z^2 - 1/30 \tag{18.13}$$

$$B_5 = z^5 - 5z^4/2 + 5z^3/3 - z/6 \tag{18.14}$$

$$B_6 = z^6 - 3z^5 + 5z^4/2 - z^2/2 + 1/42 \tag{18.15}$$

$$B_7 = z^7 - 7z^6/2 + 7z^5/2 - 7z^3/6 + z/6 \tag{18.16}$$

To use one of these polynomials as an iterated function to create a fractal, we use the technique described earlier where z_{n+1} is set equal to the polynomial, with z_n substituted for each of the zs in the polynomial, and a complex constant c is added at the end of the polynomial. The resulting equation is iterated as many times as is necessary.

Plate 21 is an example of a sixth-order Bernoulli Julia-like fractal. The parameters used to create this fractal were $XMax = 1.185$, $XMin = 0.77$, $YMax = -0.284375$, $YMin = -0.5775$, $P = -0.11$, and $Q = 0.476875$. The Random Julia coloring scheme was used.

PLATE 21   Sixth-order Bernoulli Julia-like fractal.

CHEBYSHEV POLYNOMIALS

There are four different kinds of Chebyshev polynomials, C_n, S_n, T_n, and U_n. Chebyshev polynomials are well known in electrical engineering because they describe the locations of poles and zeroes for creating frequency filters, but relatively little has been done in using these polynomials to create fractals. If there is a connection between the fractal pictures generated from these equations and filter response characteristics, it hasn't yet been fully investigated mathematically.

The following are the second-order through seventh-order Chebyshev C polynomials:

$$C_2 = z^2 - 2 \tag{18.17}$$

$$C_3 = z^3 - 3z \tag{18.18}$$

$$C_4 = z^4 - 4z^2 + 2 \tag{18.19}$$

$$C_5 = z^5 - 5z^3 + 5z \tag{18.20}$$

$$C_6 = z^6 - 6z^4 + 9z^2 - q2 \tag{18.21}$$

$$C_7 = z^7 - 7z^5 + 14z^3 - 7z \tag{18.22}$$

Plate 22 shows an expanded Julia-like Chebyshev C fifth-order fractal using the Gradient coloring scheme. The parameters are $XMax = -0.47649$, $XMin = -0.5290$, $YMax = 0.2082$, $YMin = 0.1755$, $P = -0.093531$, and $Q = 0.115$.

PLATE 22   Fifth-order Chebyshev C Julia-like fractal.

The following are the second-order through seventh-order Chebyshev S polynomials:

$$S_2 = 2z^2 - 1 \tag{18.23}$$

$$S_3 = z^3 - 2z \tag{18.24}$$

$$S_4 = z^4 - 13z^2 + 1 \tag{18.25}$$

$$S_5 = z^5 - 4z^3 + 3z \tag{18.26}$$

$$S_6 = z^6 - 5z^4 + 6z^2 - 1 \tag{18.27}$$

$$S_7 = z^7 - 6z^5 + 10z^3 - 4z \tag{18.28}$$

The following are the second-order through seventh-order Chebyshev T polynomials:

$$T_2 = 2z^2 - 1 \tag{18.29}$$

$$T_3 = 4z^3 - 3z \tag{18.30}$$

$$T_4 = 8z^4 - 8z^2 + 1 \tag{18.31}$$

$$T_5 = 16z^5 - 20z^3 + 5z \tag{18.32}$$

$$T_6 = 32z^6 - 48z^4 + 18z^2 - 1 \tag{18.33}$$

$$T_7 = 64z^7 - 112z^5 + 56z^3 - 7z \tag{18.34}$$

Plate 23 shows an expanded Chebyshev T Julia-like fractal using a random coloring scheme.

The following are the second-order through seventh-order Chebyshev U polynomials:

$$U_2 = z^2 - 2 \tag{18.35}$$

$$U_3 = 8z_3 - 4z \tag{18.36}$$

$$U_4 = 16z^4 - 12z^2 + 1 \tag{18.37}$$

$$U_5 = 32z^5 - 32z^3 + 6z \tag{18.38}$$

$$U_6 = 64z^6 - 80z^4 + 24z^2 - 1 \tag{18.39}$$

$$U_7 = 128z^7 - 192z^5 + 80z^3 - 8z \tag{18.40}$$

LEGENDRE POLYNOMIALS

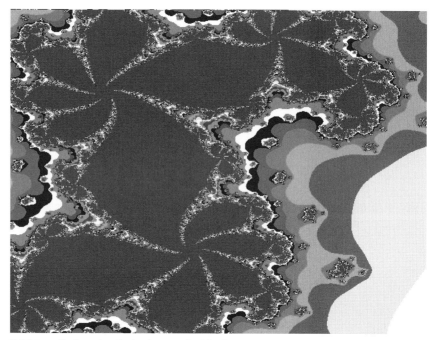

PLATE 23   Sixth-order Chebyshev *T* Julia-like fractal.

Legendre polynomials arise in describing spherical and elliptical harmonics. The fourth-order Legendre polynomial generates a rather interesting fractal, which is reminiscent in shape of the Mandelbrot set except that having a body and one "head," it has a body with five successively smaller "heads" attached. Plate 24 shows this fractal. The following are the second-order through seventh-order Legendre polynomials:

$$P_2 = 3z^2/2 - 1/2 \tag{18.41}$$

$$P_3 = 5z^3/2 - 3z/2 \tag{18.42}$$

$$P_4 = 35z^4/8 - 30z^2/8 + 3/8 \tag{18.43}$$

$$P_5 = 63z^5/8 - 70z^3/8 + 15z/8 \tag{18.44}$$

$$P_6 = 231z^6/16 - 315z^4/16 + 105z^2/16 - 5/16 \tag{18.45}$$

$$P_7 = 429z^7/16 - 693z^5/16 + 315z^3/16 - 35z/16 \tag{18.46}$$

Plate 25 shows a seventh-order Legendre Julia-like fractal.

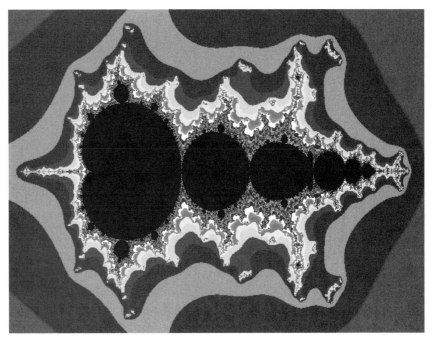

PLATE 24   Legendre fourth-order fractal.

LAGUERRE POLYNOMIALS

Laguerre polynomials arise in the process of solving the equation:

$$\int_0^\infty e^{-x} f(x)dx = \sum_{i=1}^n w_i f(x_i) + R_n \qquad (18.47)$$

The following are the second-order through seventh-order Laguerre polynomials:

$$L_2 = z^2/2 - 2z + 1 \qquad (18.48)$$

$$L_3 = -z^3/6 + 3z^2/2 - 3z + 1 \qquad (18.49)$$

$$L_4 = z^4/24 - 2z^3/3 + 3z^2 - 4z + 1 \qquad (18.50)$$

$$L_5 = -z^5/120 + 5z^4/24 - 10z^3/6 + 5z^2 - 5z + 1 \qquad (18.51)$$

$$L_6 = z^6/720 - 20z^5 + 5z^4/8 - 10z^3/3 + 15z^2/2 - 6z + 1 \qquad (18.52)$$

$$L_7 = -z^7/5040 + 7z^6/720 - 7z^5/40 + 35z^4/24 - 35z^3/6 + 21z^2/2 - 88z/9 - 1 \qquad (18.53)$$

Plate 26 shows a seventh-order Laguerre Julia-like fractal using a Gradient coloring scheme.

PLATE 25 Seventh-order Legendre Julia-like fractal.

HERMITE POLYNOMIALS

The Fractals program allows you to create fractals using the second-order through seventh-order Hermite polynomials as iterated equations. These polynomials are as follows:

$$H_2 = 4z^2 - 2 \tag{18.54}$$

$$H_3 = 8z^3 - 12z \tag{18.55}$$

$$H_4 = 16z^4 - 48z^2 + 12 \tag{18.56}$$

$$H_5 = 32z^5 - 160z^3 + 120z \tag{18.57}$$

$$H_6 = 64z^6 - 480z^4 + 720z2 - 120 \tag{18.58}$$

$$H_7 = 128z^7 - 1344z^5 + 3360z^3 - 1680z \tag{18.59}$$

PLATE 26   Seventh-order Laguerre Julia-like fractal.

As described earlier, to use one of these polynomials as an iterated function to create a fractal, z_{n+1} is set equal to the polynomial (with z_n substituted for each of the zs in the polynomial), the result is multiplied by a complex constant c, and 1.0 is added. The resulting equation is iterated as many times as is necessary.

Plate 27 is an example of a seventh-order Hermite polynomial Julia-like fractal. The parameters used to create this fractal were *XMax* = 0.165, *XMin* = −0.375, *YMax* = 0.1575, *YMin* = −0.1575, *P* = 0.0405, and *Q* = 0.030833.

PLATE 27　Seventh-order Hermite Julia-like fractal.

REFERENCES

[Abramowitz64] Abramowitz, Milton, and Stegun, Irene A., *Handbook of Mathematical Functions with Formulas, Graphs, and Mathematical Tables*, National Bureau of Standards, 1964.

CREATING YOUR OWN SECOND-ORDER TO SEVENTH-ORDER EQUATIONS

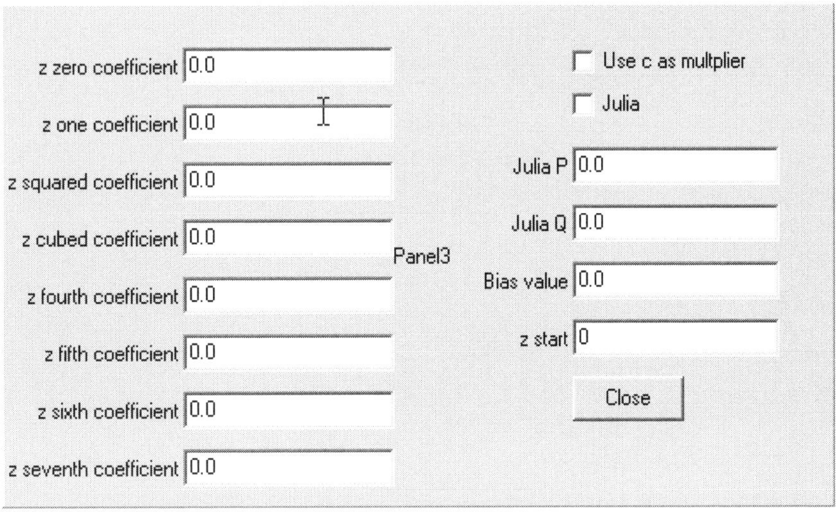

z zero coefficient 0.0

z one coefficient 0.0

z squared coefficient 0.0

z cubed coefficient 0.0

z fourth coefficient 0.0

z fifth coefficient 0.0

z sixth coefficient 0.0

z seventh coefficient 0.0

Panel3

☐ Use c as multplier

☐ Julia

Julia P 0.0

Julia Q 0.0

Bias value 0.0

z start 0

Close

Once you've become familiar with creating fractals from orthogonal polynomials, you can graduate to creating your own equations by selecting *Create 2nd to 7th Order Equation* from the *Select Fractal Type* menu. When you do this, the display shown in Figure 19.1 appears.

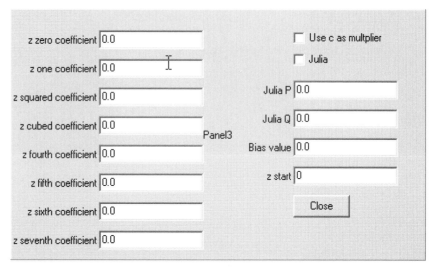

FIGURE 19.1 Display for creating second-order to seventh-order equations.

Before you begin to fill in this display, you should go to the top of the screen and fill the boxes *XMax, XMin, YMax,* and *YMin* with the values you want for the limits of the new fractal. Also, if you're going to create a Julia-like display, fill the boxes *Julia-Dragon P* and *Q* with the values you want for the real and imaginary parts that you want for the constant *c*. Then you can fill in the appropriate parameters in the display. First, you need to decide whether the complex number *c* will be added to the polynomial or whether it will be used as a multiplier for the whole polynomial. If the latter, you should check the box *Use c as multiplier*. You also need to decide whether you want to produce a Mandelbrot-like fractal or a Julia-like fractal. If Julia is your choice, check the box marked *Julia*. If you choose to produce a Mandelbrot-like set and your equation is not going to have a z^0 term, you'll need to include a number in the box marked *Bias Value;* if you don't, each set of iterations will end up with a zero value and you'll get a blank screen instead of a fractal picture. Now you are ready to create the desired polynomial by typing the coefficients into the boxes for the powers of *z* that you want to define. You must type these in as floating-point numbers. If you mess them up or insert garbage, the Fractal program will stop running when you close out this display. When you have all the coefficients set as you desire, click on *Close* to create and display the fractal that you have defined. We suggest that you get used to this process by first inserting the parameters for one of the polynomials that we looked at in previous chapters. When you've done this several times, and the fractals you defined using this process look like those produced by selecting that type of fractal from the *Select Fractal Type* menu, you should be sufficiently experienced that you can start defining your own polynomials.

Using this display, you can create any equation of up to seventh order and use it as a basis for iteration to create a fractal. However, not every equation results in an interesting fractal when iterated. In many cases, you will get a blank screen or some other very uninteresting display. As a starting point, your best bet is to try using orthogonal equations from some standard reference book of mathematical formulas. Moreover, for most equations, either using c as a multiplier or using c as a constant will produce a good fractal, but the other is apt to be disappointing. Usually one or the other of these cases produces good fractals, but not both. If you begin to create fractals that you like using these techniques, you can then make minor modifications of the parameters to fine-tune them to their best representations. Finally, if you create a fractal that you really like, be sure to record all of the parameters; you'll then be able to reproduce it when you run the program again. The parameters that you enter in the display will remain there until you change them or until you close down the program. Then they are gone forever.

PHOENIX CURVES

In the past few chapters, we have seen how lovely fractal pictures can be created by working with an iterated equation like this:

$$z_{n+1} = f(z_n) \qquad (20.1)$$

where z is a complex number. We can multiply $f(z_n)$ by a complex number c, or add c to the function, depending on which creates a more interesting fractal. We can create Mandelbrot-like fractals by letting the initial value of z be (0.0, 0.0) for each set of iterations and letting c take the value represented by each pixel of the display, or we can create Julia-like fractals by assigning c some constant value and letting the initial value of z for each set of iterations be the pixel value. For all our equations, $f(z_n)$ uses the current value of z to obtain a new value of z_{n+1}, which will then be inserted into the function for the next iteration. Now, we are going to try something a little different. Instead of limiting $f(z)$ to the current value of z, we will allow it to use both the current value of z and the value from the previous iteration. The resulting equation in its generalized form looks like this:

$$z_{n+1} = z_n{}^a + pz_n{}^b + qz_{n-1} \qquad (20.2)$$

where p is the real part of c and q is the imaginary part of c and a and b are arbitrary exponents. However, the form of the equation that yields the most interesting fractals is one which sets a to 2 and b to zero. The resulting equation is as follows:

$$z_{n+1} = z_n{}^2 + p + qz_{n-1} \qquad (20.3)$$

Shigehiro Ushiki at Kyoto University discovered this equation, which, when computed with a Julia-like technique and properly colored, looks like a pair of phoenixes. The phoenix is a mythical bird that, when burned, emerged fully grown from its ashes. To make the phoenixes look correct, the Fractal program needs to interchange the x and y coordinates of the display; otherwise, the phoenixes would be lying on their sides.

RELATIONSHIP OF MANDELBROT-LIKE AND JULIA-LIKE PHOENIX CURVES

We have seen with previous fractals that the Mandelbrot-like fractal can be used as a sort of map where cusps can be selected as points from which to create interesting Julia-like fractals. This is not true of the previous equation. You can create a Mandelbrot-like representation of the Phoenix equation, but it is not a very interesting fractal, and more significant, it doesn't possess the property of being a map of interesting

Phoenix curves. The Julia parameters selected for the Phoenix curve are
$P = 0.56667$ and $Q = -0.5$. If you found this point on the Mandelbrot representation of the Phoenix equation, it would be in the middle of a solid
area and not near any of the cusps of the curve. These parameters do not
correspond to a cusp on the Mandelbrot-like representation of the
Phoenix equation. Apparently, the mapping capability just doesn't apply
when the equation contains elements from two previous iterations of the
equation instead of just one. If you're good at mathematics you might
want to try coming up with an explanation for this.

At any rate, we haven't included the capability to produce a Mandelbrot-like representation of the Phoenix in the Fractal program. When
you select *Phoenix* from the *Select Fractal Type* menu, and then click on
Phoenix, the true Phoenix curve is displayed. This is a Julia-like curve.
Plate 28 shows a Phoenix curve that was generated using these parameters.

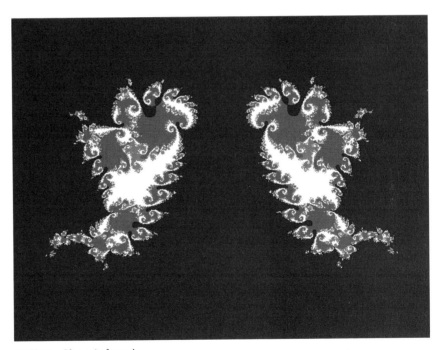

PLATE 28   Phoenix fractal.

Phoenix Fractal Coloring

This is a good point to reiterate the methods that we have been using to
color our displays. The methods used for Mandelbrot sets, Julia sets, and
the original Phoenix curve are summarized in Table 20.1.

Table 20.1 Coloring Techniques

TYPE OF FIGURE	BACKGROUND COLOR	OTHER COLORS
Mandelbrot Set	All points that do not blow up during the stated number of iterations.	Cycle through available colors for number of iterations required for blowup.
Julia Set	All points that blow up to infinity during stated number of iterations.	Cycle through a specified number of colors for ranges of value of result after iterations are complete.
Phoenix Fractal	All points that do not blow up during stated number of iterations.	Three colors: first for blow-up in 1 to 32 iterations; second for blowup in 33 to 64 iterations; third for blowup in more than 64 iterations.

You can use any of the available color combinations, but the one designed particularly for the Phoenix curve gives the most Phoenix-like representation. You will note that it is unlike any coloring technique that we have used for other fractals.

When you select *Phoenix* from the *Select Fractal Type* menu, then click on *Phoenix 2,* the Phoenix curve is generated with a different set of colors. The same technique of using four colors based on the number of iterations before the blow-up threshold is used, but the four selected colors are golds and silver and the background is peppered with random white dots to give the appearance of a night sky.

21

THE MANDELA AND POKORNY FRACTALS

S o far, all of our iterated equations have involved functions that used positive exponents of z. In this chapter, we're going to look at the kinds of fractals that we can produce when negative exponents are involved. We'll start with the Mandela curve, a fractal curve discovered by Richard Hughes. The iterated equation is as follows:

$$z_{n+1} = 1/z_n^2 = z_n^{-2} \tag{21.1}$$

In other words, at each iteration we are taking the reciprocal of z^2. The first thing to note about this curve is that there is no complex constant involved. You'll remember that to create Mandelbrot-like fractals, for each set of iterations associated with a particular pixel we let the value of the constant c be equivalent to the pixel value. We just can't do this without a constant present, so this type of curve cannot have a Mandelbrot-like equivalent. We can, however, create a Julia-like equivalent because the Julia-like curve sets z equal to the pixel value.

COLORING THE MANDELA CURVE

Most of the available coloring schemes, if applied to the Mandela curve, yield very uninteresting displays consisting of concentric circles. To create the beautiful and unusual Mandela fractal, a different way of using the colors is necessary. Remember that the Julia set is colored by cycling through the available colors, according to the value of the iterated function if the function did not exceed a specified threshold during the stated number of iterations. To create the Mandela coloring technique, the color is set according to the value of the real part of the complex iterated function for cases where the function did not exceed the stated threshold during the stated number of iterations. This seemingly insignificant variation dramatically changes the colors in the fractal display. Plate 29 is a picture of the Mandela fractal. You can duplicate this by selecting *Mandela* from the *Select Fractal Type* menu. You can also expand the display as you desire. You can choose various color combinations, but you need to remember that no matter what color combination you select, the same technique of determining colors according to the value of the real part of the iterated function continues to take place. If you want to see a beautiful variation of this fractal, choose the *Gradient* coloring scheme and then expand the interesting part of the display.

PLATE 29   Mandela fractal.

POKORNY FRACTALS

The Mandela fractal is a very specialized case of a more general iterated equation. This equation is as follows:

$$z_{n+1} = 1/(z_n + c)^m = (z_n + c)^{-m} \tag{21.2}$$

You'll note that if you run a Julia version of this with $m=2$ and $c=(0.0, 0.0)$ you should get the Mandela fractal. However, you can't get the unique Mandela coloring in this way. The default version of the Pokorny fractal is a Mandelbrot-like fractal with $m=1$. You can generate this using the Fractal program by simply selecting *Pokorny* and then *Pokorny* again from the *Select Fractal Type* menu. The resulting fractal is shown in Plate 30. Note how different this is from the Mandelbrot set, with a distinctly curvilinear triangle shape and filled with a number of circles. There is a box at the right of the Fractal program display, which is labeled *Pokorny Exponent*. The default value in this box is 1, but you can enter any number, and then run *Pokorny* again to view the new fractal. Plate 31 shows the result of setting the exponent to three and using the Complex 3 color combination. The fractal now takes the shape of a number of pointed structures surrounding a circle. Trying a few different exponents, you'll discover that the number of pointed structures surrounding the circle is *2m + 1*, where *m* is the exponent selected.

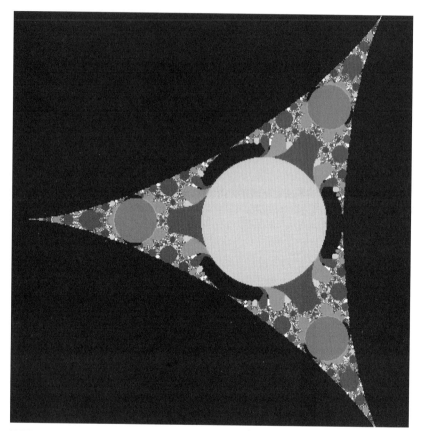

PLATE 30   Pokorny fractal with exponent 1.

You can experiment with enlarging the Pokorny fractals by clicking on a point in the fractal and then dragging to create a rectangle that will become the boundary of the enlarged fractal, or by inserting new values into the four boundary boxes at the top of the display. You can also right-click on some point of the Pokorny fractal to create a Julia-type Pokorny fractal. You can enlarge the Julia-type Pokorny too. If you use new values in the boundary boxes, when you finish inserting your new values, you'll need to click on the menu item *Repeat* to generate the new fractal display.

PLATE 31   Pokorny fractal with exponent 3.

FRACTALS USING CIRCLES

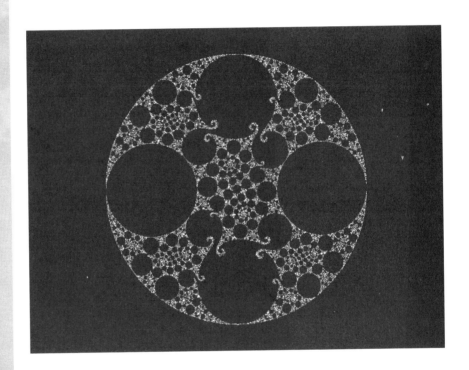

We've seen in previous chapters that we can use straight line patterns with repeated line or node replacement to create interesting and complex fractals and that we can iterate certain types of equations to produce fractal patterns of extreme complexity and beauty. Now we are going to look at fractals that are produced through the repeated use of circles. We'll give a couple of examples of patterns where the insertion of circles produces empty spaces where smaller circles can be inserted and these in turn provide additional spaces for the insertion of even smaller circles. Inherently, such patterns have the characteristic of self-similarity that is typical of fractal curves. If we got complex and beautiful curves just using straight lines, we might suspect that we could use circles, which are geometric figures of a greater order of complexity, to generate fractals that are even more interesting. This turns out be true, but determining the geometry required to put together such fractal patterns of circles and determining their radii and their coordinates involves complicated procedures that have barely been explored. You won't find much in the literature on this subject. In this chapter, we'll show you how to draw three representative fractals using circles. You will observe that we have to use some geometric formulas that rarely occur in geometry books, and when they do, they're not always clearly explained.

APOLLONIAN PACKING OF CIRCLES

This is one of the most basic of fractal curves involving circles. First, we draw three circles, each of which is externally tangent to the other two. The result of their joining is a *curvilinear triangle*. Next, we draw the circle that will fit into the curvilinear triangle, being tangent to each of the three given circles. This yields three more, smaller, curvilinear triangles. In a similar manner, we draw a circle in each of these triangles, tangent to the three circles that make up the triangle. As a result, for each curvilinear triangle, three more smaller curvilinear triangles are generated. These in turn can be filled with smaller circles. Continuing the process indefinitely yields the ultimate fractal curve, but practical programming considerations suggest that we stop the process after thirteen or fourteen iterations; before too long, the circles become so small that they either appear on our screen as dots, or not at all. It can be shown that the resulting curve is fractal and has a Hausdorff-Besicovitch dimension (discovered by Boyd) of approximately 1.3058.

This begs the question of how to perform this repeated circle-drawing task. Provided we can figure out how to draw a circle within a curvilinear triangle, knowing the coordinates of the center and the radius of each of the three circles that generate the curvilinear triangle, then we can use a recursive process similar to that we have used for previous fractals to draw repeated circles. However, this is a difficult mathematical problem. Using the principles of analytic geometry, if we know the position of the center of a desired circle and its radius, we can determine the x and y coordinates of the new circle. But how do we get these needed pieces of information?

SODDY'S FORMULA

It turns out that there is a formula for the radius of the circle inscribed within the curvilinear triangle, given solely in terms of the radii of the three circles that make up the triangle. It is called *Soddy's formula* [Soddy36]. One form of this formula is this expression:

$$2(1/a^2 + 1/b^2 + 1/c^2 + 1r^2) = (1/a + 1/b + 1/c + 1/r) \qquad (22.1)$$

where a, b, and c are the radii of the three given tangent circles and r is the radius of the circle that is to be drawn tangent to the three given circles. The form of expression that we will work with is as follows:

$$1/r = 1/a + 1/b = 1/c + 2\sqrt{(1/bc + 1ac = 1/ab)} \qquad (22.2)$$

Once we know the radius of the circle to be drawn and the radii and center coordinates of the three given circles, we can do some complicated but straightforward mathematics to determine the x and y coordinates of the center of the circle to be drawn. We can then draw the circle.

CREATING THE APOLLONIAN CIRCLE PACKING FRACTAL

Until this point, we have been able to generate our fractals using either the L-Systems approach or through a Fractal subroutine that performs an iteration process. Neither of these techniques works with the Apollonian packing of circles; we have to have a completely separate set of subroutines to perform the mathematics just described and the recursion needed to produce the desired fractal. These are included in the Fractal program. You just need to choose *Circles* from the *Select Fractal Type* menu and then click on *Apollonian*. The fractal that will be generated will have the recursion level shown in the box at the right of the screen labeled *Select Fractal Level* (the default level is 5). To see how this fractal is created, you can start with a level of 1 and work upward. Figure 22.1 shows the Apollonian Packing fractal at level 1, Figure 22.2 shows level 2, Figure 22.3 shows level 3, Figure 22.4 shows level 4, Figure 22.5 shows level 5, and Figure 22.6 shows level 6. Finally, Plate 32 shows the Apollonian Packing of Circles at level 12 in full color. You can enlarge a portion of this fractal by clicking at the top left corner that you want for the new fractal and then dragging to the bottom right corner. When you release the mouse button, the enlarged fractal will be drawn. Alternatively, you can put new limits for an expanded fractal in the *XMax, XMin, YMax,* and *YMin* boxes and then click on *Repeat* to create an expanded fractal.

FIGURE 22.1   Apollonian packing of circles fractal at level 1.

FIGURE 22.2   Apollonian packing of circles fractal at level 2.

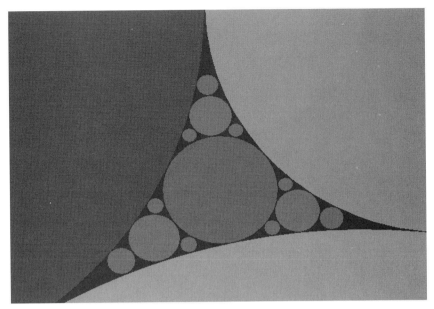

FIGURE 22.3   Apollonian packing of circles fractal at level 3.

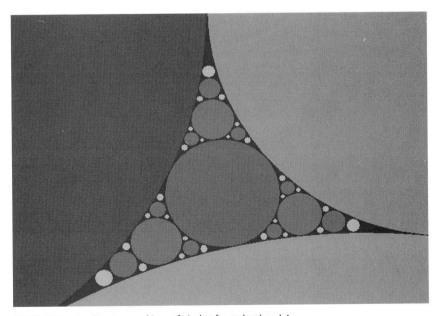

FIGURE 22.4   Apollonian packing of circles fractal at level 4.

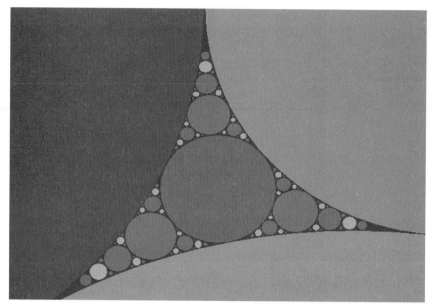

FIGURE 22.5 Apollonian packing of circles fractal at level 5.

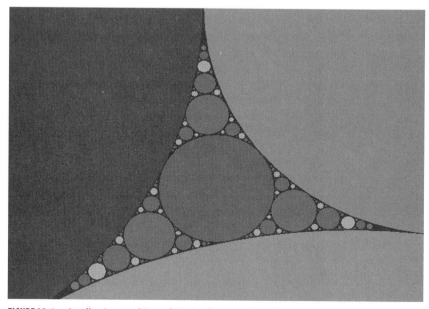

FIGURE 22.6 Apollonian packing of circles fractal at level 6.

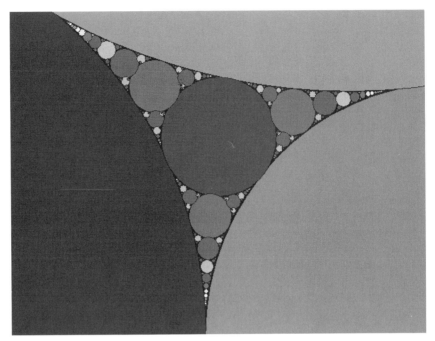

PLATE 32 Appolonian packing of circles.

INVERSION

In producing fractal curves involving circles, an interesting mapping technique can transform a fairly simple pattern of circles into a much more interesting one. The technique also has uses in geometry, where it can often simplify complex relationships so that proofs of theorems become much simpler. The technique is called *inversion* and it uses a given circle to map all the points on a plane to different locations on the plane, except for the point at the very center of the circle. The mapping is done as follows:

1. A line is drawn from the center of the circle (O) to the point to be mapped (P).
2. The new mapped point P' is placed on the line OP so that the product of the distances OP and OP' is equal to the square of the radius of the circle, r^2.

Inversion has several interesting properties. They include the following:

1. Any circle whose circumference passes through the center of the reference circle, O, maps into a straight line parallel to the tangent through the circle being mapped at O.
2. Any circle that is orthogonal to the circle of inversion inverts into itself.

3. Any other circle maps into a circle but at a different location and different radius.

4. You might suspect that if a circle maps into another circle, the center of the first circle would map into the center of the new circle, but this is not true. If you want to perform an inversion and then plot it on the screen, you cannot successfully use data from the original circle to determine the center and radius of the mapped circle and then draw it using this information. You must map every point on the circle to its new location and plot it there.

PHARAOH'S BREASTPLATE

Pharaoh's Breastplate is the name given by Mandelbrot to a figure created using a pattern of circles with inversion. Plate 33 shows the Pharaoh's Breastplate without inversion. The two large circles represent the final reference circles. These only are mapped by inversion resulting in the upper and lower parallel horizontal lines. The other circles are tangent to each other and to the horizontal lines. They can extend as far to the left and right as you want them to. These circles are all defined in the program by simple mathematical relationships.

To obtain the Pharaoh's Breastplate with inversion, we apply the inversion process to every point on the figures shown in Plate 33 except the two large reference circles and their inversion lines. The result is shown in Plate 34. The software in the Fractal program that does this is much more complicated than that needed to create the display without inversion. Note that for these fractals you cannot change the colors nor enlarge the fractals.

SELF-HOMOGRAPHIC FRACTALS

We've just seen how an interesting fractal can be created by using the mapping technique called *inversion*. Other mapping techniques can also be used to produce beautiful and interesting fractals. In particular, we are going to look at a technique where we begin with a point in the complex plane and apply a transformation to it to yield another point, which is at another location on the plane. We apply the same transformation again to the new point and obtain a third one. After we have done this a sufficient number of times, the result of the aggregate of points is a lovely fractal, provided the initial point and transformation parameters were chosen suitably. The most general form of the mapping we shall use is

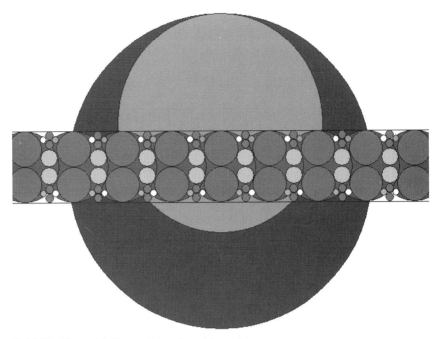

PLATE 33   Pharaoh's Breastplate without inversion.

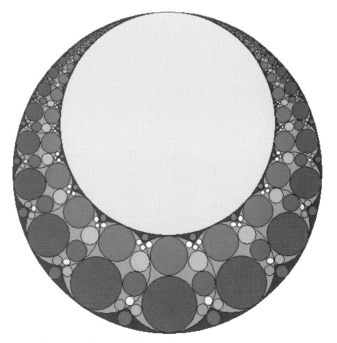

PLATE 34   Pharaoh's Breastplate with inversion.

$$T(z) = \frac{az + b}{cz + d}$$

(22.3)

where

$$ad - bc = 1$$

(22.4)

This transformation is known as the Mobius map or sometimes as the fractional linear transformation. If we start with a single point on the z plane and apply the transformation, it maps into another point on the plane. Using recursion, we repeat this process a number of times, resulting in a beautiful fractal, whose complexity increases as we approach the limiting case for this transformation. Our Fractal program requires three inputs *T1, T2,* and *T4,* which are traces. We use these to create the transformation. You can create this fractal by choosing *Circles* from the *Select Fractal Type* menu, and then choosing *Self-homographic* from the submenu that appears. Another submenu then appears that gives you a number of choices of the values of *T1* and *T2*, each of which creates a different fractal. Plate 35 shows the most complex of these fractals. You can use the *Select Color Combination* menu, and select *Color Background* to change the background color for the fractal. You can either choose one of the preset colors or choose *Select Background Color,* which brings up a display from which you can choose the exact color that you want for the background. For the image color, the program cycles through a group of colors as the recursion level changes. If you choose the *Select Color Combination* menu and then select *Image Color,* you can then select the color that is to be first in the group chosen for recycling [Mumford02].

REFERENCES

[Mumford02] Mumford, David, Series, Caroline, and Wright, David, *Indra's Pearls,* Cambridge University Press, 2002.
[Soddy36] Soddy, F. "The Kiss Precise." *Nature* (1936): Vol. 137, p. 1021.

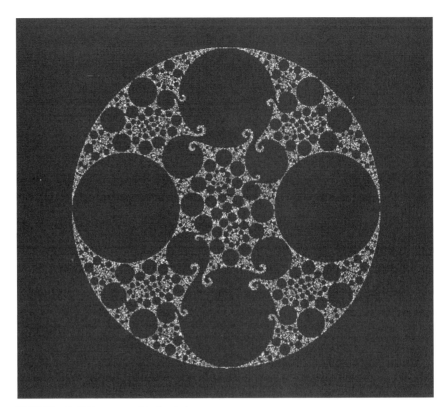

PLATE 35   Self-Homographic fractal.

BARNSLEY FRACTALS

Michael Barnsley, while a professor at Georgia Institute of Technology, discovered a number of interesting techniques for creating fractals. His book, *Fractals Everywhere*, provides a wealth of fractal information [Barnsley88]. One type of fractal in the book, which we shall demonstrate in this chapter, uses an iteration process in which one of two iteration processes is used for the next iteration, depending on the value of z after each iteration. The resulting fractals are much different in appearance from any we have seen so far. We are going to look at three of these fractals, and a representation of the well-known Sierpinski triangle using this technique.

THE FIRST BARNSLEY FRACTAL

The first Barnsley fractal is defined as follows:

$$z_{n+1} = cz_n - c \text{ when the real part of } z_n \geq 0$$
$$= cz_n + c \text{ otherwise} \tag{23.1}$$

Previously, we stated that for various fractals using iteration, if the value of z ever reached or exceeded 2.0, the ultimate value of z if iteration continued would reach infinity. Thus, we were safe in stopping the iteration process if a maximum size of 4.0 was ever reached (allowing some cushion for accumulated errors). Because of the way that the Barnsley fractal moves back and forth between two iteration equations, it never blows up to infinity. Fortunately, in testing whether to stop the process of iterating a Barnsley fractal, the test of stopping iteration when z reaches or exceeds 4.0 works very well, even though this no longer implies that z will go to infinity. Plate 36 shows the first Barnsley fractal. You can enlarge this fractal by setting the cursor to the point where you want the top left corner of the expanded fractal to be and then holding down the left mouse button while you drag the cursor to where you want the bottom right corner. When you release the mouse button, the enlarged fractal will be drawn. You can also change the bounds of the fractal by entering new values into the boxes labeled *XMax, XMin, YMax,* and *YMin* at the top of the screen. When you've entered the new values, click on the menu item *Repeat* to draw the fractal with the new bounds.

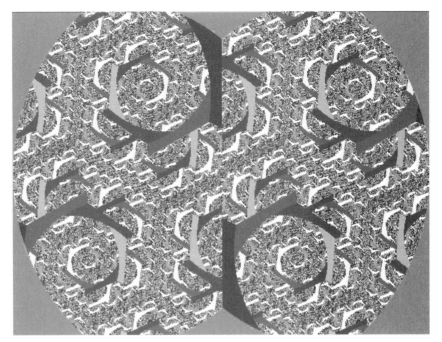

PLATE 36   First Barnsley fractal.

The Second Barnsley Fractal

The second Barnsley fractal is defined as follows:

$$z_{n+1} = cz_n - c \text{ when the imaginary part of } cz_n \geq 0$$
$$= cz_n + c \quad \text{otherwise} \tag{23.2}$$

Note that the two formulas used for iterating to the next value of z are identical with those used for the first Barnsley fractal, but the test for determining which to use is different. For the first Barnsley fractal, the test is based on the value of the real part of cz_n, whereas for the second Barnsley fractal, the test is based on the value of the imaginary part of cz_n. Plate 37 shows the second Barnsley fractal. You can enlarge or change the bounds of this fractal in the same way as described earlier for the first Barnsley fractal.

PLATE 37   Second Barnsley fractal.

THE THIRD BARNSLEY FRACTAL

The third Barnsley fractal is defined as follows:

$$z_{n+1} = z_n^2 - 1.0 \qquad\qquad \text{when the real part of } z_n \geq 0$$

$$z_{n+1} = z_n^2 - 1.0 + p\ real(z_n) \qquad \text{otherwise} \qquad\qquad (23.3)$$

If we just look at the first alternative of this equation, we might suspect that we'd get something very similar to the Mandelbrot set as the result of our iteration process. However, the seemingly minor change of adding another term to the equation when the real part of z is less than zero gives us a new fractal that is quite different from anything we've seen before. This fractal can also be expanded or its bounds changed as described for the first Barnsley fractal. The resulting fractal is shown in Plate 38.

PLATE 38   Third Barnsley fractal.

THE BARNSLEY SIERPINSKI TRIANGLE

We've already seen several ways of generating the Sierpinski triangle fractal. Here is another way that uses the Barnsley technique of using different equations for iteration, depending on the value of the current iteration of z. The equations involved are as follows:

$$z_{n+1} = 2z_n - i \qquad \textit{when the imaginary part of } z_n > 0.5$$

$$z_{n+1} = 2z_n - 1 \qquad \textit{when the real part of } z_n > 0.5$$

$$z_{n+1} = 2z_n \qquad \textit{otherwise} \qquad (23.4)$$

This fractal is interesting because of how we use two tests to alter the iteration equation. The basic iteration equation is $z_{n+1} = 2z_n$. We first test whether the imaginary part of z_n is greater than 0.5. If this is true, we subtract i (imaginary unit) from the iteration equation. If the first test is not true, we run a second test to determine if the real part of z_n is greater than 0.5. If this is true, we subtract 1 from the iteration equation. Plate 39 shows the resulting Sierpinski triangle. Like the other Barnsley fractals, it can be expanded or the bounds altered by using the same techniques.

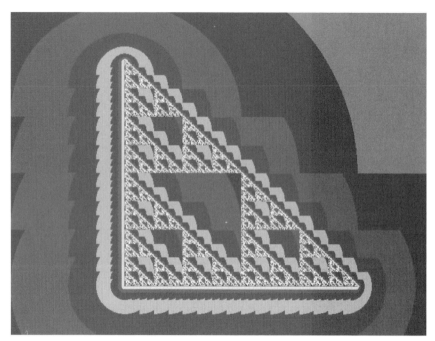

PLATE 39 Barnsley Sierpinski triangle fractal.

References

[Barnsley88] Barnsley, Michael, *Fractals Everywhere*. Academic Press, Inc., 1988.

ichael Barnsley, the discoverer of the Barnsley fractals, also discovered what he calls Iterated Function Systems or, in a joking
mode, the Chaos Game [Barnsley88]. Suppose we have a function that can be used to rotate, scale, or translate a point. We apply this
function repeatedly in an iterative manner—that is, the new point obtained by the first iteration has the function again applied to it an so on.
We've already seen that contrary to the intuitive idea that the result will
be a completely random distribution of points, such processes can result
in well-defined figures. Barnsley's contributions to this branch of science
are determining the functions needed to produce some very interesting
figures and the development of techniques for discovering functions that
can be used to save photos or artwork with very large compression ratios.

AFFINE TRANSFORMATIONS

The primary tool used in generating particular graphics with Iterated
Function Systems (IFS) is the affine transformation. This is a function
that looks like the following:

$$\begin{bmatrix} x_{n+1} \\ y_{n+1} \end{bmatrix} = \begin{bmatrix} a & b \\ c & d \end{bmatrix} \begin{bmatrix} x_n \\ y_n \end{bmatrix} + \begin{bmatrix} e \\ f \end{bmatrix} = \begin{bmatrix} ax + by + e \\ cx + dy + f \end{bmatrix} \qquad (24.1)$$

The parameters a, b, c, and d perform a rotation. Furthermore, the
setting of the magnitudes of these parameters may result in a scaling such
that the distance between points can increase, decrease, or remain the
same. (For the IFS to work properly, the scaling must always result in the
distance between points decreasing. This kind of transformation is called
a *contraction*.) The parameters e and f cause a linear translation of the
point being operated on. Hence, the entire function causes a geometric
figure being operated on to be translated to a new location, and there ro-
tated and shrunk to a smaller size. Table 24.1 shows the parameter values
that are used to create seven different IFS displays. You'll note that an IFS
display contains two or more sets of transforms. The probability of each
set being selected for a given iteration is given by the associated parameter p. The resulting pictures appear in Figures 24.1 through 24.7 respectively.

Table 24.1 Affine Transformation Parameters

FIGURE	A	B	C	D	E	F	P
Fern Leaf	0.0	0.0	0.0	0.16	0.0	0.0	0.01
	0.2	−0.26	0.23	0.22	0.0	0.2	0.07
	−0.15	0.28	0.26	0.24	0.0	0.2	0.07
	0.85	0.04	−0.04	0.85	0.0	0.2	0.85
Sierpinski	0.5	0.0	0.0	0.5	0.0	0.0	0.3333
Triangle	0.5	0.0	0.0	0.5	1.0	0.0	0.3333
	0.5	0.0	0.0	0.5	0.5	0.5	0.3333
Tree	0.0	0.0	0.0	0.5	0.0	0.0	0.05
	0.1	0.0	0.0	0.1	0.0	0.2	0.15
	0.42	−0.42	0.42	0.42	0.0	0.2	0.4
	−0.42	0.42	−0.42	0.42	0.0	0.2	0.4
Kantor	0.333	0.0	0.0	0.333	0.0	0.0	0.3333
Tree	0.333	0.0	0.0	0.333	1.0	0.0	0.3333
	0.667	0.0	0.0	0.667	0.5	0.5	0.3333
Maple	0.35173	0.35537	−0.35537	0.35173	0.3545	0.5	0.1773
Leaf	0.35338	−0.3537	0.35373	0.35338	0.2879	0.1528	0.380
	0.5	0.0	0.0	0.5	0.25	0.462	0.1773
	0.50154	−0.0018	0.00157	0.58795	0.2501	0.1054	0.2091
	0.00364	0.0	0.0	0.57832	0.5016	0.0606	0.0562
Dragon	0.450	−0.5	0.4	0.55	0.0	0.0	05
	0.450	−0.5	0.4	0.55	1.0	0.0	05
von Koch	0.333	0.0	0.0	0.333	0.0	0.0	0.25
Snowflake	-0.167	−0.289	0.289	0.167	0.333	0.0	0.25
	0.167	0.289	−0.289	0.167	0.5	0.289	0.25
	0.333	0.0	0.0	0.333	0.667	0.0	0.25

FIGURE 24.1   IFS fern leaf.

FIGURE 24.2   IFS Sierpinski triangle.

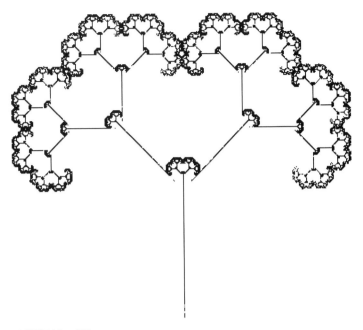

FIGURE 24.3   IFS tree.

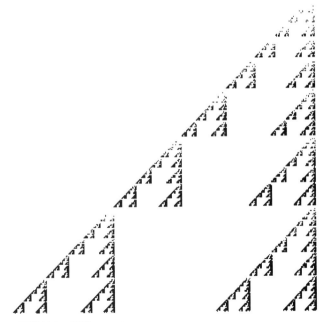

FIGURE 24.4   IFS kantor tree.

FIGURE 24.5   IFS maple leaf.

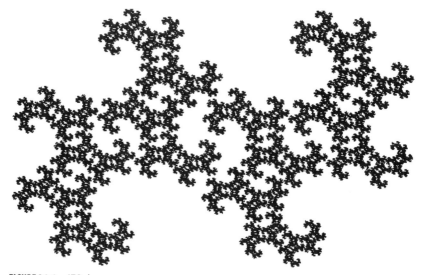

FIGURE 24.6   IFS dragon.

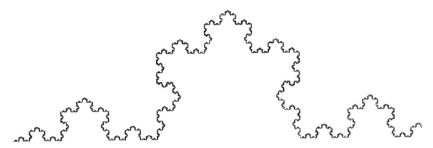

FIGURE 24.7   IFS von Koch snowflake.

You'll note that there are two IFS fractals that you've seen before, drawn by L-Systems techniques, the Sierpinski triangle and the von Koch snowflake. The von Koch snowflake drawn by the IFS technique shows the pattern that is drawn for only one side of the snowflake. To see the complete snowflake, use the L-Systems technique, which draws the IFS snowflake on each of the three sides of a triangle. As you get deeper into the study of fractals, it is important to note that identical fractals can be generated by two such diverse techniques.

A modern PC can generate most of the IFS fractals described in this book almost instantaneously. This doesn't provide any clues about the order in which points are generated as the picture is being created. To make this visible to the viewer, the Fractals program intentionally introduces a large amount of delay after each point is created. Thus, you can see the IFS fractal slowly growing on your screen until it finally reaches its completed form.

THE COLLAGE THEOREM

By now, it should be evident that some very beautiful and intricate pictures can be created by using the IFS technique with just a few simple transforms. However, we can't tell, as yet, how these transformations were determined. The collage theorem is central to IFS design. The mathematics is rather complicated, but basically the theorem states that if you have a graphic that you want to produce with the IFS technique, if you can cover the graphic with smaller copies of itself with no holes or overlapping, the fractal produced by using these small copies as transforms with the IFS technique will always look exactly like the original graphic. This gives you some guidelines for creating IFS transformations, but still leaves a lot to your imagination. The book *Fractal Imaging* by Ning Lu, a member of Barnsley's staff, provides information and some software that can be used for converting images into a group of fractal transformations from which the original graphic can be re-created [Lu 97].

CREATING YOUR OWN IFS FRACTALS

Looking at the values in Table 24.1, you might get the idea that it would be very simple to create your own special fractals by just choosing the right coefficients. A lot of experimentation is often required to get just the right set of transformations to create a good quality picture. The fractals shown in Figures 24.1 through 24.7 are the result of much trial and error by those working in this field. If you want to try creating your own fractals, you can select *Iterated Function Systems* from the *Select Fractal Type* menu and then *Create Your Own IFS* from the submenu that appears. The display shown in Figure 24.8 will then appear.

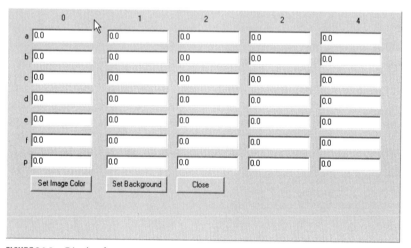

FIGURE 24.8   Display for creating your own IFS fractals.

You can see that this display allows you to fill in as many as five sets of parameters and probabilities. Then, by clicking the *Set Image Color* box, you can select the color in which you want the fractal to be displayed, and by clicking the *Set Background* box, you can select the desire background color. When you've got everything the way you want it, click on *Close* and the fractal will be drawn. Try this first with a couple of the parameter sets from Table 24.1. When you feel comfortable with this, try changing the parameters. Fortunately, after you have created a fractal with this technique, all the information you entered is stored so that if you don't like the result, you can call the *Create Your Own IFS* display again and make any changes to your original data without having to reenter everything.

REFERENCES

[Barnsley88] Barnsley, Michael, *Fractals Everywhere.* Academic Press, Inc., 1988.

[Lu97] Lu, Ning, *Fractal Imaging.* Academic Press, Inc., 1997.

MIDPOINT DISPLACEMENT
FRACTALS

From our investigations of L-Systems fractals, we are familiar with the technique of starting with a initiator consisting of a simple geometric figure such as a triangle or a square, replacing each line with a new line pattern called the generator, and then repeating this process a number of times to create a complex fractal graphic. In this chapter, we are going to investigate a similar but different technique that is a great way to produce sections of terrain such as mountains. To do this, instead of replacing line segments in our basic geometric figure, we are going to find the midpoint of each line segment and draw lines connecting the midpoints. Figure 25.1 shows the result of the first iteration of this process. We now have four smaller triangles enclosed within the original larger triangle.

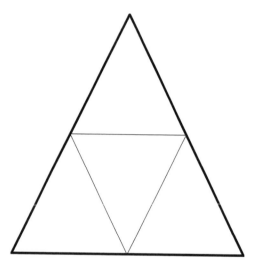

FIGURE 25.1   First step in subdividing a triangle.

MIDPOINT DISPLACEMENT

It's possible to perform additional iterations using this process to subdivide each of the four small triangles into four triangles that are smaller yet, until the triangles become so small that they cannot be resolved by the computer display. The result is truly a fractal, but a rather uninteresting one. Now suppose that instead of drawing lines between midpoints, we randomly perturb each midpoint in the y direction and then draw the midpoint connecting lines. Two things need to be considered during this process. First, the amount of random perturbation must be proportional to the size of the triangle; otherwise, after several iterations the perturbations are apt to be greater than the length of the triangle sides themselves. This is accomplished by multiplying a properly scaled random number by the length of the side whose midpoint has been obtained. Thus, as triangles get smaller, so does the perturbation. Second, it is a good idea to avoid random numbers close to zero, which would result in no perturbation at all. To do this, we create a way of generating random numbers that produce numbers between some lower and upper limit, but can be either plus or minus the random number value. This allows the perturbation to be either in the plus or minus y direction, but never be close to zero. A typical result for the first iteration step is shown in Figure 25.2 and a typical result for the second iteration step is shown in Figure 25.3.

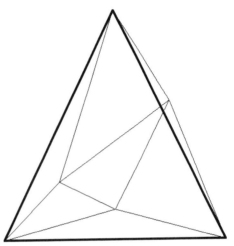

FIGURE 25.2   First iteration with randomly perturbed midpoints.

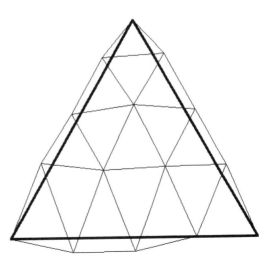

FIGURE 25.3   Second iteration with randomly perturbed midpoints.

TRIANGLES WITH A COMMON LINE

There is only one trouble with the process just described. During multiple subdivisions, there are likely to be cases where two triangles have one line in common. When the two triangles are subdivided, the random perturbation of the common line is likely to be different for each of the two triangles. If this resulted in the subdivided triangles overlapping each other we could probably live with it, but if a space is left between the two perturbed midpoints for the common line, we will end up with a noticeable and objectionable space between the subdivided triangles. Figure 25.4 illustrates this phenomenon.

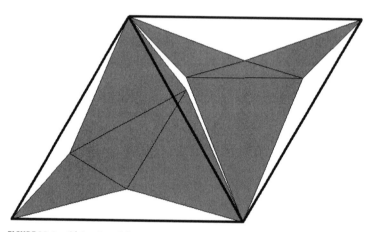

FIGURE 25.4   Objectionable space created when midpoint of a common line is randomly displaced for two triangles.

This illustration should make clear that it would be highly desirable for each perturbation of a common line to be identical. This can be achieved by setting up a seed for the random number generator that is derived from the coordinates of the ends of the line to be subdivided. For two calculations for a common line (both endpoints being identical), the seed will be the same, so the same random number will be generated and the perturbation will be the same. Figure 25.5 gives the result of this process, showing that the objectionable gaps have been removed.

MIDPOINT DISPLACEMENT IN THE FRACTAL PROGRAM

While running the Fractal program, you can use the *Select Fractal Type* menu to select the fractal type *Mountain*. This gives a typical example of using midpoint displacement fractals to represent a mountain range. Four

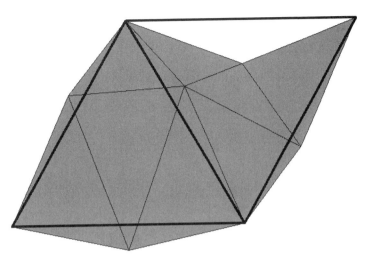

FIGURE 25.5   Result of subdividing two triangles when the same perturbation is used each time a common line is processed.

triangles are used to start the process. You can select *Wire Frame,* which draws all the lines that make up the triangles, or *Filled,* which fills each triangle with a color. The menu allows iteration levels of 1 to 5 and a *Select Level* option, which chooses as the iteration level the number inserted into the *Select Fractal Level* box at the right of the screen. The Fractal program includes obtaining a random number that is obtained when it begins generating the Mountain fractal and is then added to the seed each time a new seed is calculated and the random generator reset to it. Each time you run the Mountain fractal, the display will be different. When you see one that you especially like, you should save it, because it is unlikely that you'll be able to obtain that same picture again.

COLORING MOUNTAINS

When the *Filled* options of the mountain are selected, the Fractal program automatically uses the Gradient coloring scheme to fill the triangles, using a default set of colors that are appropriate to how mountains might look. After generating a mountain fractal, the user can click on *Modify Gradient,* which can be used as described in Chapter 15 to change the mountain colors. The display that appears, in addition to providing complete control of the gradient coloring, has two boxes. One, labeled *Set Default Gradient,* allows you to return to the original set of gradient colors used by all other fractal types. The other, labeled *Set Mountain Gradient,* allows you to return to the default set of gradient colors used by the mountain fractal display. Plate 40 shows an example of a Mountain factal.

PLATE 40   Mountain factal.

RANDOM NUMBER CONSIDERATIONS

So before each midpoint perturbation, the random number generator is started with a new seed, and then a random number is used to control the perturbation. Are these, then, really random numbers? Well, actually, they are not. They are really a fixed set of numbers that are related to an equation involving endpoints. Although this is a mathematical truth, the results we get using this technique are quite good and can produce some very interesting landscapes.

FURTHER CONSIDERATIONS

You can do many things with this general technique, but they haven't all been included in the Fractal program. A completely different bunch of landscapes could be created by using squares or hexagons as the initial shapes to be subdivided. An almost unlimited number of different methods of coloring methods are also available. The mountains created by the program are simply typical examples of a technique that you might want to apply in greater detail.

ABOUT THE CD-ROM

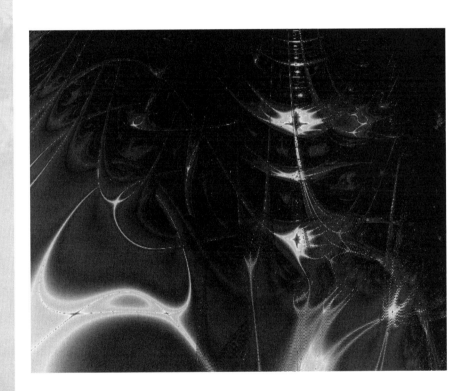

FOLDERS

CreatingFractals–Pictures: Contains all of the figures from the book.
Fractal Pictures: Contains a number of particularly interesting fractal images.
Fractals: Contains the source code for the Fractal program.

THE FRACTAL PROGRAM

The CD-ROM will install the programs you need to run the Fractals program on any computer using Microsoft Windows. When you insert the CD-ROM in your computer, the installation program should begin to run automatically. If it does not, run the program Setup.exe from the CD-ROM.

You will then see a screen that allows you to choose *No Questions Asked Installation* or *Advanced Options Installation*. If you choose the first option, only the Fractals program will be installed on your hard drive, along with a shortcut to it indicated by a fractal icon on your desktop. Once you have performed this installation, you'll be able to run the program any time you want to and create any of the thousands of different fractals that you might like to view and/or save.

If you select the second option, your display will show you four icons labeled *New Component*. As you click your cursor on each of these, a note at the bottom of the screen will show you what will be installed if that icon is activated. Initially, only the first icon is activated, as shown by a check mark. This automatically causes the installation program to install the Fractals program in the same way that was described above for the *No Questions Asked Installation*.

CREATING FRACTALS - PICTURES

The directory *CreatingFractals-Pictures* includes a subdirectory for each chapter of the book that has figures. Each subdirectory contains all of the figures for that chapter in Windows *.bmp* format. All of the color plates are also included. Please be aware that you can access all of these pictures and view them from the CD-ROM. The second *New Component* icon described above will allow the installation process to transfer all of these files to your hard drive. They will be in the *My Documents* directory. You can select this option by checking the box to the left of the second icon. Don't do this unless you have plenty of space available on your hard drive, as they use up a lot of memory.

FRACTAL PICTURES

The directory *Fractal Pictures* contains a number of interesting fractal pictures. Many of these have rather long file names, which you can use to re-create the picture with your fractal program. For example, one of these pictures has the file name *Ber5J.37+.055+.4865+.2406+1.36+ .2625.bmp*. To reproduce this fractal you would select the fractal type *Bernoulli 5 Julia*. You would then set the parameters at the top of the Fractals display screen as follows: *XMax* = 0.37, *XMin* = 0.055, *YMax* = 0.4865, *YMin* = 0.2406, *P* = 1.36, and *Q* = 0.2625. Your fractal will then be reproduced using the default coloring scheme. If the fractal picture from the CD-ROM uses a different coloring scheme and you want to duplicate it, you'll need to find the coloring scheme by trial and error as this isn't included in the file name. Please be aware that you can access all of these pictures and view them from the CD-ROM. The third *New Component* icon described above will allow the installation process to transfer all of these files to your hard drive. They will be in the *My Documents* directory. You can select this option by checking the box to the left of the third icon. Don't do this unless you have plenty of space available on your hard drive, as they use up a lot of memory.

FRACTALS SOURCE CODE

Finally, the directory *Fractals* contains all of the source code needed to modify and recompile the *Fractals.exe* program if you own a copy of Borland C++ Builder 6.0 or higher. Using these files, you can modify the Fractals program to meet your exact requirements. This directory will be installed under the *My Documents* directory. The *Fractals.exe* program included in this directory is the same as what is automatically installed using the *Setup* program, so if you have any problems with your installation of the Fractals program, you can manually transfer this program to your hard drive instead of doing the automatic installation. Note, however, that if you recompile using Borland C++ Builder, the program *Fractals.exe* will then include any changes you have made and will no longer be identical to that included in the Setup program. Normally to use this directory with Borland C++, you will have to install it on your hard drive by checking the box to the left of the fourth *New Component* icon. It will be installed under the *My Documents* directory. If you have no intention of delving into the source code, don't bother to do this. You can always transfer these files to a directory of your own choosing at a later time.

It is important that you read the file *README*, on the CD-ROM as this outlines the license that you are granted, showing you what you can and cannot do with the CD-ROM.

System Requirements

The Fractal program should install and run on any computer running Windows 98 or higher. All of the computers that the author used to test this program had at least 128 megabytes of memory, but the program should run equally well on computers having at least 16 megabytes of memory. For the Fractal program itself, about 3 megabytes of hard disk space are required. Of course, if you are going to take advantage of the options to load the sample picture files and figures to your hard drive, considerable additional space is required.

INDEX